Wrestling with God

Wrestling with God

Paul O. Ingram

Cascade Books
A division of *Wipf & Stock Publishers*
199 West 8th Avenue, Suite 3 • Eugene OR 97401

WRESTLING WITH GOD

Cascade Books
A Division of Wipf & Stock Publishers
199 W. 8th Ave., Suite 3
Eugene, OR 97401

ISBN: 1-59752-495-6

Cataloging-in-Publication Data:

Ingram, Paul O., 1939–

    Wrestling with God / Paul O. Ingram

        xii + 116 p.; 23 cm.

        Includes bibliographical references.

        ISBN 1-59752-495-6   (alk. paper)

        1. Christianity and other religions. 2. Christianity and other religions—Buddhism. 3. Buddhism—Relations—Christianity. 4. Religious pluralism. I. Title.

BR128 I54 2006

Contents

Preface

My favorite text in the Pentateuch is the story of Jacob's wrestling match with God at the Brook of Jabbok:

> And Jacob was left alone; and a man wrestled with him until the breaking of the day. When the man saw that he did not prevail against Jacob, he touched the hollow of his thigh; and Jacob's thigh was put out of joint as he wrestled with him. Then he said, "Let me go, for the day is breaking." But Jacob said, "I will not let you go until you bless me." And he said to him, "What is your name?" And he said, "Jacob." Then he said, "Your name shall no longer be Jacob, but Israel, for you have striven with God and with men and have prevailed." Then Jacob asked him, "Tell me, I pray, your name." But he said, "Why is it you ask my name?" And there he blessed him. So Jacob called the name of the place Peniel, saying "I have seen God face to face, and yet my life is preserved." The sun rose upon him as he passed Peniel, limping because of his thigh. (Gen 32:24-31)

Thus did Jacob the wrestler become Israel: "he who wrestles with God" and wins.

I have long thought that the story of Jacob's combat with God at Jabbok is a paradigm for the journey of faith. According to biblical tradition, there is never a time when God is not present in creation or in human history, so there is never a time when we are not encountering God, even if we are not conscious of the encounter. But consciousness of God's presence invariably initiates a struggle that can be bruising. In Christian experience, the life of faith is always a struggle that engenders what Luther called "theology of the cross" because faith calls us, like it called Abraham, to a journey that takes us beyond the safe conventionalities of cultural and social boundaries. Faith is God's way of starting a fight with us. A hip—or something else—will be thrown out of joint and we will limp through the remainder of our lives. Yet like limping Jacob, we are not defeated even as our wrestling match with God leaves us with scars.

In its original context in the Pentateuch, the story of Jacob's encounter with God at the Brook of Jabbok is a central paradigm for the Jewish community's wrestling match with God through the Torah, God's "instructions" given to the people of Israel through Moses on Mount Sinai. God's Torah instructs people about how to live with justice and compassion toward all human beings as well as in harmony with nature. But it's one thing to be chosen by God to live according to the Torah so as to be a "light to the nations," as the prophet Isaiah put it. It's quite another thing to figure out *how* to guide one's life in accordance with the Torah's commandments. So in imitation of Jacob, Jewish history is a never-ending wrestling match with God to figure out what the Torah means and how to implement it in Jewish life. It is for this, according to the Exodus traditions, that Israel was "chosen": to wrestle with God through study of the Torah as interpreted through the lenses of rabbinic opinion in the Mishnah, Gemara, and Talmud.

The struggle to be God's "Chosen People" has cost the Jews dearly, for no religious community has suffered as much persecution as have Jews. Atrocities committed against the Jewish community by Christians have their origins in the anti-Judaism of the New Testament.[1] After the fourth century, Christian anti-Judaism was transformed into Christian anti-semitism, the beginning of a sixteen-hundred-year history of persecution that is so violent that the survival of the Jewish community seems itself an argument for the existence of God. Not even the Holocaust could extinguish Judaism's light to the nations.

The story of Jacob's wrestling match with God at Jabbok has also been a paradigm for Christians. Jürgen Moltmann, caught up in the terrors of the end of World War II, wrestled with God to survive the abyss of his participation in the war's senselessness and his guilt about the Jewish death camps. He emerged from his confinement in a prisoner of war camp in Scotland "limping." His wrestling match with God continues through the discipline of theological reflection.[2] For Moltmann, the story of Jacob's fight with God is a paradigm of the life of Christian faith.

There is an odd thing about this story. Jacob doesn't quit even after God dislocates his hip. Jacob just keeps wrestling, refusing to stop until God blesses him. But while not defeated by God, he will walk with a limp for the rest of his life. According to St. Paul, the life of faith is initiated by God and both Jewish and Christian experience is evidence that faith does not make one's life easier, but harder. As there's no cheap grace in Jacob's encounter with God, so there is no cheap grace in the Christian experience of Christ. Of course, my particular wrestling match with God has not been as dangerous, and certainly not as profound, as Jacob's or my Jewish brothers' and sisters' or Moltmann's. Yet the life of faith, I think, entails a life of struggle for all faithful persons. And like Jacob at Jabbok, wrestling with God in faith will not defeat us, provided we don't let go. But the fight will leave us limping. Nor will the struggle of faith ever come to an end while we are alive. So like Annie Dillard, "Sometimes I ride a bucking faith while one hand grips and the other flails in the air, and like any daredevil I gouge with my heels for blood, for a wilder ride, for more."[3]

My ride began forty years ago and was given its first public expression in 1997 when I published a book entitled *Wrestling with the Ox: A Theology of Religious Experience*.[4] In this book I appropriated the Ten Ox Herding pictures from the Zen Buddhist tradition as a metaphor for the themes I wanted to address. The Ten Ox Herding pictures are a symbolic portrayal of the ten stages of Awakening as portrayed in Mahayana Buddhist teachings. Each picture provided the title and themes for the ten individual chapters of the book. My colleagues in the Department of Religion at Pacific Lutheran University were particularly helpful critics when I wrote this book, both in terms of clarifying the reason for writing *Wrestling with the Ox* and clearly formulating the issues with which I was concerned as I wrote: (1) conceptualizing a Christian pluralistic theology of religious experience primarily in dialogue with Buddhism, but also in conversation with Confucian, Taoist, Hindu, Jewish, and Islamic traditions, and (2) specifying how the academic discipline called history of religions might be put to use as a form of theological reflection to help Christians advance in their own faith journey.

Consequently *Wrestling with the Ox* evolved into a description of various theological options that might be appropriate for Christians as they interact in dialogue with non-Christians. While I am pleased with this book, the process of writing it brought to light unresolved questions regarding my own particular Christian faith and practice. Once again, my colleagues urged me to reflect on these unresolved questions in another book. So, inspired by Jacob's fight with God at the Brook of Jabbok, *Wrestling with God* is a theological reflection on these unresolved questions. My overall contention is that Christianity is now in a process of decay and that dialogue with the world's religions—especially Buddhism—and Christian dialogue with the natural sciences are the two most important intellectual foci for thinking Christians. My thesis is that through such dialogue Christians can hope for the emergence of new forms of faith and practice that are relevant to the complexities of contemporary life.

Writers need critical readers. I am particularly grateful to K. C. Hanson, who is chief editor of Cascade Books, for publishing *Wrestling with God*, and for the encouragement of another editor at Cascade Books, David Root, whose enthusiastic support for this project was evident from the earliest days of its writing. In particular, David asked very penetrating questions in regard to areas that needed my clarification, and I have carefully listened to his suggestions and critique with gratitude. Heather Carraher did wonderful service as a proofreader. To all of these generous people at Cascade Books goes my deepest appreciation for their professionalism.

An English major from Pacific Lutheran University deserves special thanks. Jacob Freeman read through the manuscript with an expert eye for typological errors and the sometimes vague sentence structures that often plague a manuscript like a Chinese Hungry Ghost. Any one who is a teacher can spot excellence in young students from a mile away. Thanks, Jacob, for all your good work.

One of the joys of my professional life is my association with seven faculty colleagues in the Department of Religion at Pacific Lutheran University. Our department has encouraged a deep sense of interdependence and mutual support for both teaching and scholarship that is unusual in academia. In regard to the writing of this particular book, these friends and colleagues have in their own particular way made it possible for me to write a better book than I could have written apart from their always focused and well intentioned criticism.

Patricia Killen, whose academic specialization is American religious history, was a very helpful source for my understanding of what she calls "the art of theological reflection," about which she has written a book[5] and which underlies one-third of the material of chapter three. She also read and commented on chapters two, four, five, and six. Writers need critical readers, and Patricia is among the best there are.

Robert L. Stivers is a specialist in Christian ethics. Bob and I have worked together for thirty years and currently co-teach a course entitled "Religion and Culture" that focuses on environmental issues and what dialogue with the world's religions can contribute to resolving the current ecological crisis. Bob's review of chapter four, where I take on issues of Buddhist and Christian social engagement, clarified for me the distinguishing character of Christian social ethics of which I had not been fully aware.

Samuel Torvend teaches European Church history as well as courses on Luther and the Reformation. His careful reading of my remarks on Luther and other aspects of church history referenced throughout this book owe much of their clarity to Sam's demand that I describe historical events and persons accurately and coherently.

Two of my colleagues in biblical studies, Douglas Oakman and Alicia Batten, offered substantial criticism and encouragement as I wrote chapter two, especially my references to the story of Jacob and God at the Brook of Jabbok and a text from the Gospel of Mark (9:33-40) that is the source of my "sermon" in chapter two. Biblical criticism is an art, and Doug and Alicia are among the more creative biblical scholars now working in North America.

Marit Trelstad and Kathlyn Breazeale, fellow graduates of the Claremont Graduate University (except that I go back further in time), have been wonderful conversation partners in process philosophy and theology. They offered substantial critique on the various elements of Whiteheadian process thought that I brought into each chapter in this book, but especially in regard to the material on the natural sciences in chapters five and six. Marit and Kathi are also first-rate feminist thinkers who made sure that I worked hard to free my worldview (and this book) from the false pretensions of patriarchal dogma in whatever form it assumes.

This book is dedicated to Patricia, Bob, Sam, Doug, Alica, Marit, and Kathi, whose collective intellect, support, and friendship through the years has felt like grace that is amazing.

Finally, my wife, Regina, a medical social worker who is theologically trained, always supports my work. I can't imagine my life as a writer without our conversations before and during the writing process.

Tacoma, Washington
December 22, 2005

ENDNOTES

[1] See Rosemary Radford Ruether, *Faith and Fratricide: The Theological Roots of Anti-Semitism* (New York: Seabury, 1979).

[2] Jürgen Moltmann, *The Source of Life: The Holy Spirit and the Theology of Life*, trans. Margaret Kohl (Minneapolis: Fortress, 1997) 1–2.

[3] Annie Dillard, *Pilgrim at Tinkers Creek* (New York: Harper and Row, 1974) 269.

[4] Paul O. Ingram, *Wrestling with the Ox: A Theology of Religious Experience* (New York: Continuum, 1997).

[5] Patricia O'Connell Killen and John de Beer, *The Art of Theological Reflection* (New York: Crossroads, 1994).

Chapter One

"Fruit Salad Can Be Delicious"

In *Living Buddha, Living Christ,* the Vietnamese Zen monk Thich Nhat Hanh described an interreligious meeting in Sri Lanka where a Christian speaker assured the audience: "We are going to hear about the beauties of several traditions, but that does not mean we are going to make a fruit salad." When it came Thich Nhat Hanh's turn to speak, he commented: "Fruit salad can be delicious! I have shared the Eucharist with Father Daniel Berrigan, and our worship became possible because of the sufferings we Vietnamese and Americans shared over many years." Thich Nhat Hanh then observed that some of the "Buddhists present were shocked . . . and many Christians seemed truly horrified." [1]

That meeting between Thich Nhat Hanh and Daniel Berrigan was a form of Buddhist-Christian dialogue. Both are ordained clergy in their respective traditions; both were at the time living in exile because of their protest of the war in Vietnam; each shared the depths of his religious life with the other. What brought them together in Sri Lanka was not just intellectual curiosity but a gift from those who suffered on all sides of the civil war in Vietnam: a sense of compassion and kinship that deepened their religious lives while transcending ideological and institutional boundaries. Such creatively transforming events are rather common experiences among Buddhists and Christians engaged in serious dialogue.

1

In my case, adding the natural sciences as a "third partner" has enriched as it has creatively transformed my theological reflection. Or restated in terms of the running metaphor of this book, this book should be read as my particular wrestling match with God, not at the River Jabbok, but within the territory of contemporary Buddhist-Christian dialogue contextualized by the natural sciences.

Because most conversations between religious persons tend to be monologues rather than dialogues, it is helpful to sketch briefly the interdependent elements that structure an interreligious dialogue.

First, interreligious dialogue is a specific type of conversation between faithful persons of different religious traditions that is without ulterior motives. Lack of ulterior motives is perhaps the most important element of genuine dialogical encounter. Dialogue is a mutual sharing between two or more persons in which one seeks to place one's faith in conversation with persons dwelling in a faith perspective other than one's own, while at the same time sharing one's own faith perspective openly and honestly. Ulterior motives of any sort, such as the conversion of another to one's own standpoint, transforms the conversation to a monological debate.

Second, genuine interreligious dialogue requires being engaged by the faith and practice of persons dwelling in religious standpoints other than our own. In such a conversation, our own standpoints are stretched, tested, and challenged by the faith and practices of our dialogical partner.

Third, interreligious dialogue requires critical and empathetic understanding of one's own standpoint. It's a bit like being in love. We can recognize the reality of another human being's love because of our own particular experiences of receiving and giving love. In a similar way, living in the depths of one's own tradition enables us to apprehend the depths of our partner's tradition. It's not possible to hear the music of another person's faith and practice unless we can hear the music of our own.

Fourth, interreligious dialogue presupposes that truth is relational in structure. It may not be quite correct to think that truth is relative, but our sense of truth is certainly relational. From scientific accounts of the physical realities underlying the universe to social scientific theory to theological explorations of humanity's religious traditions, we can only understand from the perspective we occupy at the moment we understand; we can only apprehend whatever truth is from the particular cultural, religious, social, gender-specific standpoints we inhabit. For this reason, Carmelite nuns practicing contemplative prayer do not ordinarily experience the Buddha nature underlying all things and events at every moment of space-time. Nor do Zen Buddhist nuns ordinarily experience mystical union with Christ the Bridegroom as the result of their meditative practice. Since no one and no religious tradition can enclose the whole of reality—the way things really are as opposed to the way we desire things to be—within its particular institutional and doctrinal boundaries, dialogue reveals that the faith and practice of another faithful human being can challenge, stretch, and enliven our particular self-awareness as religious persons. In other words, the purpose of interreligious dialogue is mutual creative transformation.[2]

Finally, the practice of interreligious dialogue requires taking risks. It is not for the spiritually timid. Openness to the insights of persons living in the depths of religious traditions other than one's own is a kind of "odyssey," which John S. Dunne described as "passing over and returning."[3] In dialogue, we cross the borders of our faith into the faith and practice of other human beings, learn and appropriate what we can, and return to the "home" of our own tradition. Most of the time, Christians who pass over into the faith and practice of Buddhists, for example, return to their own Christian perspective changed and enriched, maintaining a Christian self-identity, but one different from the self-identity experienced before passing over. The same process happens for Buddhists in dialogue with Christians. The risk is that one's faith and worldview are transformed in unpredictable ways. Sometimes, persons crossing over to another religious tradition remain there. Sometimes persons experience multiple religious identities. The practice of interreligious dialogue is not for persons who easily lose their nerve.

Those engaged in serious dialogue learn early that generalizations about Buddhism and Christianity, or about Buddhists and Christians, are difficult and dangerous. Still, the need for generalization is necessary, provided one is aware that there are always exceptions. One such generalization is that Buddhists and Christians often practice dialogue for different reasons. Accordingly, in the following section of this chapter I have briefly described the three major forms of dialogue that have evolved in contemporary Buddhist-Christian encounter: conceptual dialogue, socially engaged dialogue, and interior dialogue. As the elements of interreligious dialogue are interdependent, so also are the forms of dialogue.

The remaining chapters of this book address ideas, issues, and practices that have evolved in my particular Lutheran-Christian perspective as a result of forty years of crossing over into Buddhist tradition and through my growing passion for dialogue with the natural sciences. Chapter two, "Alicia's Koan," is my answer-in-process to a question a student asked me a few years ago: "If there is only one God, why are there so many religions?" Part of my answer to this koan has emerged from my studies in history of religions in general and from my continuing conceptual dialogue with Buddhism in particular. The focus of conceptual dialogue is doctrinal, theological, and philosophical; it concerns a religious tradition's self-understanding and worldview. In conceptual dialogue, Buddhists and Christians compare theological and philosophical formulations on such questions as "ultimate reality," human nature, suffering and evil; nature and ecology; salvation/liberation; the relation between love, compassion and justice; the role of Jesus in Christianity and the role of the Buddha in Buddhism; and what Christians and Buddhists can learn from each other.

Chapter three, "On the Practice of Faith," is about interior dialogue. Interior dialogue is concerned with the interaction between Buddhist and Christian spiritual practices. Here, I have concentrated on the interdependence of conceptual, socially engaged, and interior dialogue, illustrated by my particular "practice" as influenced by Buddhist traditions of meditative discipline and Christian centering prayer. Chapter three's thesis is that interior dialogue opens Buddhists and Christians to the possibilities for understanding, appreciating, and appropriating insights from both traditions in a process of mutual creative transformation.

Historically, conceptual dialogue has been especially emphasized by Christian participants in contemporary Buddhist-Christian encounter because Christians inherit a long tradition of theological reflection as a means of structuring practice, which is not to say that socially engaged and interior dialogue are absent from Christian encounter with Buddhism.[4] In Christian language, this tradition is called "faith seeking understanding," and it is one of the reasons that Christian theology places heavy importance on doctrinal and conceptual clarity in a way not usually emphasized by non-Christian traditions. Yet many dialogically engaged Christians locate themselves as heirs of a tradition that has, as a whole, lost credibility and relevance within the context of contemporary religious and secular pluralism. For them, the task is to apprehend theological formulations that respond to these challenges.

This is a major interest of process theologian John Cobb's conceptual dialogue with Buddhism, especially with noted Buddhist philosopher Masao Abe. Cobb has appropriated Buddhist doctrines of impermanence, "non-self," and interdependence into his understanding of God as a means of helping Christians recover biblical insights about human nature and God that are more relevant to contemporary life and experience. He is noted for his claim that "a Christian can be a Buddhist, too."[5]

Conceptual dialogue has been of interest to Buddhists as well. Masao Abe is the best known member of the "Kyoto School" of Japanese philosophy, mostly composed of Zen Buddhists trained not only in the abstractions of Mahayana Buddhist dialectics but also in the traditions of German philosophy, particularly Kant and Hegel. More than any other Buddhist I know, Abe comprehends and appreciates the complexities of Christian theological tradition. He senses that Christian tradition has a long history of working for social and economic justice as a central form of its practice, and he thinks Buddhists have much to learn from Christians about the struggle for justice within the rough-and-tumble of political and economic existence.

Conceptual dialogue has clearly demonstrated the need to confront issues of economic, social, and ecological injustice. These issues are global, interconnected, interdependent, and are not specific to any one religion or culture. The interdependence of interior and socially engaged dialogue is the topic of chapter four.

Chapter five, "On Buddhist-Christian Dialogue with the Natural Sciences," is a reflection on the possibilities for Buddhist-Christian mutual transformation through conceptual dialogue with the natural sciences. Chapter five's thesis is that contemporary scientific descriptions of the natural forces at play in the universe's origins and Darwinian descriptions of biological evolution have generated a common origin story accessible to persons in all religious traditions. Accordingly, this chapter's topic is about how bringing the natural sciences into Buddhist-Christian conceptual dialogue as a third partner might creatively transform both traditions and argues that current Big Bang cosmology leaves room for a notion of God—conceptualized primarily in terms of Whiteheadian process theology—as creator and sustainer of the universe.

Chapter six asks "Is This All there Is?" in light of contemporary scientific cosmology. Given what contemporary cosmologists are now beginning to theorize about the final destiny of the expanding universe of which we are a part, I argue that the answer to this question is "no," and that there are rational grounds for hope that the universe as God's created order is evolving toward an eschatological fulfillment beyond anything scientific descriptions of physical processes would in themselves lead us to imagine.

On Theological Reflection in a Religiously Plural World

Since this book was written as the theological reflection of a Lutheran in dialogue with Buddhism contextualized by the natural sciences, I had better come clean about one of the presuppositions that will run throughout these chapters. My favorite analogy for understanding the practice of Christian theological reflection comes from Luther's reading of the doctrine of the Incarnation. This doctrine holds that Jesus was both human and divine. This paradoxical meeting of the two natures supplies the metaphor by which Christians are taught to understand the many interdependent paradoxes of human experience: flesh and spirit, nature and grace, God and Caesar, faith and reason, justice and mercy. When emphasis is placed on the divine at the expense of the human—the fundamentalist error—Jesus becomes an ethical authority and teacher of rules who is remote from our experience. When Jesus is thought of as merely human—the liberal error—he is nothing more than a model social worker or pop guru.

One could ask why the incarnational balance of the human and the divine is not so obvious to human beings, especially to many Christians, as to be universally accepted. The truth is that human beings find it difficult to live with paradox. Especially in Western cultures that tend to be rooted in Aristotle's logic of non-contradiction, it seems much easier to seek a resolution in one direction or another, and indeed, making such a choice often seems like the most principled option. But the second-century Buddhist logician, Nagarjuna, whispers a warning to Christians who have ears to hear: "form is emptiness, emptiness is form," which I interpret to mean that the historical Jesus is divinity in history, divinity in history is the historical Jesus. While I do not think that divinity in history *only* manifests itself in the historical Jesus, the historical Jesus is the focal point of Christian apprehension of God within the rough-and-tumble of historical existence. Accordingly, the historian of religions side of my Lutheran theological identity requires a brief discussion about "religious pluralism," by which I mean that Christian tradition is one among many religions traditions through which human beings have structured human existence. While this book is intended to be a Christian theological reflection, it asserts that "truth sufficient for salvation" is not limited to Christian experience, and my starting point is what John Hick called the "pluralist hypothesis."

Although Hick's "pluralistic hypothesis," which is discussed more fully in chapter two, has drawn strong criticism, something similar to this theory has bubbled beneath my theological reflection from the moment I enrolled in my first history of religions course forty years ago at Chapman University. But I didn't have a name for it until I read Hick's *An Interpretation of Religion*.[6] While I do not particularly care for the Kantian epistemology that underlies Hick's version of the pluralist hypothesis, I do think the essentials of his views are similar to my own.[7]

One way of imagining the version of the pluralistic hypothesis that will operate in this book is the wave-particle complementarity in contemporary quantum physics. In certain experimental situations, light can be observed to have either wave-like properties or particle-like properties, depending on "how" one is observing photons. There appears to be no line separating wave-like behavior and particle-like behavior in the photon itself. As Ian Barbour describes Niels Bohr's complementarity principle, "No sharp line can be drawn between the process of observation and what is observed,"[8] because photons exhibit both wave and particle characteristics, though not simultaneously. It all depends on whether the observer is measuring a photon's location or velocity, neither of which can be measured, as far as anyone now knows, simultaneously. Something similar, I think, is going on with humanity's religious traditions, all of which take place within the limitations of historical and cultural contexts. That is, meditation, doctrinal reflection, prayer, social engagement, chanting, and communal liturgy are how particular religious communities "observe" the Sacred.

Yet I must also acknowledge that important criticisms have been leveled against any version of the pluralist hypothesis. For example, some scholars view pluralist theologies as a product of post-Western Enlightenment rationalism and thereby link theological pluralism with a capitalist world hegemony. This seems to be the heart of many post-modernist critiques. They argue that pluralist theologies arise within particular elite social groups and institutions and that support for such theologies conceals exploitive political and religious agendas.[9]

Furthermore, pluralist understandings of humanity's religious traditions presuppose that there exists some principle of unity underlying the diversity of human beings, that there is a common human essence that defines all human beings as "human." This too, it is argued, is the offspring of the Western Enlightenment that imposes an illegitimate Western claim about what religious experience ought to be for everyone. Thereby, pluralism is merely another form of out-of-date Western cultural political and economic hegemony,[10] at bottom "just another expression of Western ideological imperialism that is in complicity with the injustice of global capitalist ideology."[11]

At the risk of sounding like an elitist white Western male capitalist oppressor, I have always found this particular critique of pluralist theology of religions rather odd. Of course, pluralist theologies do have in common an awareness of global interdependency. It's also true that Western Europe and the United States share major responsibility for the current unjust and dangerous division of this planet into a rich "first-world" minority and a "second" and "third-world" majority held in degrading poverty by the free-market capitalism of the United States and Western Europe. But Western complicity in world-wide economic injustice applies also to Western theological exclusivists and inclusivists, as well as to post-modernists and everyone else in Western society or elsewhere in the world—even those working for world peace or against racism. Pointing the finger at Western theological pluralists for this situation is as unfair as it is logically untenable.

Related to post-modernist criticism of theological pluralism is the charge that pluralist accounts of the world's religious traditions are different from those accounts each particular tradition gives of itself, which implies that pluralists are intolerant of religious diversity. For in seeing the religious traditions of humanity as different culturally and historically limited responses to one Sacred Reality, religious pluralists seem to dismiss uncritically the differences between religious traditions. This appears to many to be an ahistorical and unjustifiable subordination of the religious traditions to an over all theory that denies the concrete character of each tradition's symbols, practices, and teachings. In short, pluralist accounts of the world's religious traditions look like another form of Western, particularly Christian, theological imperialism.[12]

This criticism of theological pluralism exposes a real issue confronting pluralist accounts of religious diversity, including my own. Yet the idea that the religious traditions of the world are culturally and historically limited responses to a single reality that each names differently does not inherently imply that all religious traditions teach the same things or are equally true or equally valid responses to the Sacred. There is much in all religious traditions that is nonsense. The truth claims of some religious traditions may be closer approximations than others, although how this could be decided is a mystery since one can only judge the universal claims of another religious tradition from the point of view of one's own universal claims. So from my understanding of religious pluralism, the world's religious traditions are most coherently interpreted as different totalities that consist of distinctive ways of conceiving and experiencing the Sacred, which, as a Christian, I happen to name God, and my Buddhist brothers and sisters happen to name differently.

Nor need a pluralist theology assert that there ought to be a global religious tradition that combines the "best" insights of particular traditions into a single unity. Instead, adherents of each existing tradition should respond as fully as possible to the Sacred in their own distinctive ways and live out their paths accordingly. Finally, a pluralist theology of religions need not assume that conflicting and incommensurable teachings in the world's religions are an illusion or can be explained away because of the way different traditions train persons to "read" the Sacred. Buddhist non-theism and Christian theism, for example, are incommensurable teachings. As opposite ontological claims about the structure of existence, only one can be true.

Yet in spite of the real incommensurability between the world's religious traditions, I have experienced the plurality of humanity's religious traditions as a resource for deepening my own religious faith and practice. Often, the differences between religious traditions have taught me as much as perceived similarities. It was reading the *Bhagavad-gita*'s theology of the many incarnations of Brahman into the deities worshiped by Hindus that helped me begin to understand the meaning of the Christian doctrine of

9

the incarnation of God in the historical Jesus as the Christ, particularly as read through the lenses of the Prologue to the Gospel of John. Writing my doctoral dissertation on Shinran's doctrine of "awakening by faith through Amida Buddha's other-power alone" clarified for me what St. Paul, Augustine, and Luther had in mind when they wrote about how humanity's relation with God is created through "justification by faith through grace alone." I think Buddhist doctrines of suffering and its causes, non-self, and interdependence are dead right, but not absolutely so. Buddhist teachings have helped me understand biblical insights into these same realities. Islam's uncompromising monotheism has forced me to think more clearly about Christian trinitarian theology as a way of avoiding the error of reducing God to that which is not God, which in Islamic teaching is called *shirk* or "idolatry." Much fundamentalist Christian talk about God seems like *shirk* to me. Christians need to pay more attention to Islamic criticism of Christian theological reflection in this regard.

Similarly, much of the criticism of pluralist theologies of religions seem to me to have a hidden agenda: imposing Christian inclusivism on non-Christian traditions by affirming that whatever truth exists in non-Christian teachings bears a family resemblance to the truths and practices most fully embodied in Christian teachings and practices. This is another version of theological imperialism in that it asserts the superiority of Christian tradition over non-Christian tradition.

Accordingly, the realities of religious pluralism have pushed my understanding of distinctively Christian theological reflection to yet another paradox: relevant Christian theology must balance an intense—if occasionally anguished—attachment to Christian tradition with openness to the world with all of its pluralism. This pluralism includes the plurality of the world's religions. This paradox is experienced as an awareness of our separation from God and the limits of human institutions coupled with the persistent hope that separation from God and from human beings in all communities, both religious and secular, can be overcome. It follows, then, that Christian theological reflection is a "practice," a "path," a "way" that one explores in dialogue with earnest seekers following non-Christian paths. Theological reflection is always an open-ended process of faith seeking understanding in which the journey—for all of us—may be more important than the destination.

A Reflection in Process on the Church's Mission

In light of the claims and arguments in this chapter and the remaining chapters of *Wrestling with God*, how should Christians understand Jesus' reported command to "go . . . and make disciples of all nations" (Matt 27:19)? In other words, how should we think about the church's mission to the world? Like every other Christian, I suppose, when I think about this issue I need to begin with my particular experience. Consequently, I must note that for the most part, students in my university courses and people attending adult education classes at local churches to which I have been invited to teach respond positively, often eagerly, to the ideas I have described in this chapter and throughout this book. That is, in my experience, they feel that such titles as "Lord," "Savior," or "only begotten Son of the Father" become more meaningful, engaging, and liberating when these titles are not construed as doctrinal litmus tests for excluding non-Christians from God's love and justice. Instead, their faith in God's saving grace at work in the universe has deepened when this same language is understood as confessional and symbolic, meant primarily to call persons to accept Jesus' challenge to work for the creation of community based on love and justice, which Jesus called "the Kingdom of God."

So when this same language is understood as "confessional" and "symbolic," meant primarily to call persons to accept the historical Jesus' message to "go and do likewise" in working for a community based on love and justice for all human beings—and I would add for all living things—regardless of the particular religious or non-religious label they wear, their faith in God's saving grace at work in the universe has deepened. In this regard, I often think that most university students and people sitting in the pews of churches are light years ahead of many pastors and denominational leaders because they intuitively understand, without any help from me, that Christian faith does not entail competition with other religious traditions because they experience daily the realities of living out their faith surrounded by the realities of religious pluralism. They seem to have learned from the historical Jesus that God doesn't give a damn about "religion"; God passionately cares about persons and the life forms with which we share this planet.

So in my particular experience, I have not found the warnings offered by some of my colleagues in the academic community and in mainline denominations to be valid or appropriate. Pursuing a pluralistic theology means that I might mislead faithful Christians and risk departing from my own faith community. In my experience, I have found that while my particular view of the theological implications of religious pluralism, which I do not claim to be the only view possible, does indeed anger some Christians, most Christian people eagerly accept a pluralistic image of Christ with openness and even gratitude, because they have long had questions about this aspect of their faith, but have never felt free to explore them. They have also felt mystified by the fact that many theologians and church leaders have not taken up their questions with sufficient candor or honesty. For me, and for many Christian friends, it seems that a Christ who is the way open to other religious ways is a Christ that can be more easily followed, and that following Christ demands a revised understanding of Christian missions in a pluralistic world.

What would such a revision look like? While it is not feasible to fully articulate a pluralistic theology of missions in this particular book, it is feasible to suggest in outline the foundational principle from which a pluralistic theology of missions might start. Stated simply, if the mission of Jesus was centered on announcing and establishing the Kingdom of God—an inclusive community centered on compassion and liberating justice from the systemic forms of oppression that affect the lives of all persons and Planet Earth itself—it cannot be otherwise for the mission of the church. Furthermore, there is general agreement among both Catholic and mainline Protestant theologians that the church and the Kingdom of God are not, and cannot be, identical. The Kingdom is not only more extensive than the Christian church, it is also more important.

So the primary reason Jesus sent out disciples in the past, which faithful Christians should imitate in the present, was not to build the church's membership rolls, although I am always pleased when someone associates with a Christian community because they have heard the music of Christian faith. My guess is that Jesus' disciples were pleased as well when this happened. The primary reason for "going into the world" is to work to build the Reign of God that is the defining character of the Kingdom of God. Of course, the reality of the Reign of God is something that happens by God's grace, and I take it as given that no one would follow the historical Jesus to this end apart from the grace of God's call to do so. I also take it as given that Christians can, and should, engage non-Christian religious traditions positively as "ways of saving grace" by which God's love and call for liberating justice are revealed to all persons by means of their own religious traditions. In other words, a pluralistic theology of missions should view non-Christian religious traditions as not only "ways of salvation" but also "ways to the Kingdom."

I need to be clear, however, that I am not espousing a variation of Karl Rahner's "anonymous Christianity," according to which, whenever non-Christians are living according to virtues Christians can recognize as valid, they are saved by the same grace Christians experience mediated through the church. In other words, non-Christians are Christians without knowing it.[13] What I *am* espousing is that Christians should think of non-Christian men and women living at the depths of their particular faith traditions as co-workers for the Kingdom of God, not as anonymous assistants or as benighted pagans in need of conversion to one of the institutionalized church denominations. Or as Paul Knitter expressed it:

> It is not just that Christians may have the *name* for what the others are searching for, but also, just as likely, the others may have the *name* for what Christians are searching for. To hold up the Kingdom of God as the Christian name for the common ground for interreligious dialogue is to call for a level playing field where everyone is ready and expected to learn and teach.[14]

ENDNOTES

[1] Thich Nhat Hanh, *Living Buddha, Living Christ* (Berkeley: Riverhead, 1995) 1–2.
[2] Paul O. Ingram and Frederick J. Streng, eds., *Buddhist-Christian Dialogue: Mutual Renewal and Transformation* (Honolulu: University of Hawaii Press, 1986) 177–94.
[3] John S. Dunne, *The Way of All The Earth* (Notre Dame: University of Notre Dame Press, 1978).
[4] For a summary of contemporary Christian theological reflection of Buddhism, see my essay "Buddhism and Christian Theology," in *The Modern Theologians*, ed. David F. Ford, 4th ed. (Oxford: Blackwell, 2005) 682–702.
[5] John B. Cobb Jr., "Can A Christian Be a Buddhist, Too?" *Japanese Religions* 10 (1979) 1–20.

[6] John Hick, *An Interpretation of Religion: Human Responses to the Transcendent* (New Haven: Yale University Press, 1989) chapter 14.

[7] For a discussion of the pluralist hypothesis as a research program for the academic discipline called "history of religions" written from the point of view of the process metaphysics of Alfred North Whitehead, see my essay "'That We May Know Each Other': The Pluralist Hypothesis as a Research Program," *Buddhist-Christian Studies* 24 (2004) 135–57.

[8] Ian Barbour, *Religion and Science: Historical and Contemporary Issues*, rev. ed. (San Francisco: HarperCollins, 1997) 167.

[9] See, for example John Milbank, "The End of Dialogue," in *Christian Uniqueness Reconsidered*, edited by Gavin D'Costa (Maryknoll, N.Y.: Orbis, 1990) 174–92.

[10] Lesslie Newbigin, *The Gospel in a Pluralist Society* (Grand Rapids: Eerdmans, 1989) 168.

[11] Kenneth Surin, "A 'Politics of Speech': Religious Pluralism in the Age of the McDonald's Hamburger," in *Christian Uniqueness Reconsidered*, edited by Gavin D'Costa, 192–212.

[12] See John B. Cobb Jr., "Beyond 'Pluralism,'" in *Christian Uniqueness Reconsidered*, edited by Gavin D'Costa, 81–95; Wolfhart Pannenberg, "Religious Pluralism and Conflicting Truth Claims," in *Christian Uniqueness*, 96–106, Jürgen Moltmann, "Is 'Pluralistic Theology' Useful for the Dialogue of World Religions," in *Christian Uniqueness*, 149–73; and "Whose Objectivity? Which Neutrality? The Doomed Quest for a Neutral Vantage Point From Which to Judge Religions," *Religious Studies* 29 (March 1993) 94.

[13] Karl Rahner, *Theological Investigations* (Baltimore: Helicon, 1978) 5:131–40.

[14] Paul F. Knitter, *Jesus and the Other Names: Christian Mission and Global Responsibility* (Maryknoll, N.Y.: Orbis, 1996) 120.

Chapter 2

Alyssa's Koan:
"Why Are There So Many Religions?"

Teaching undergraduates to think critically about religious experience is a great gig, especially when one of them shows up at your office with that gleam in her eyes that says "I want to talk about this." At such moments one's students become "hidden teachers," as Loren Eisley phrased it,[1] because the energy and focus of their questions force one to reexamine ideas germinating in one's mind over a long academic career. Such moments do not happen often in the field of religious studies. When they do, usually after intense intellectual and emotional struggle, insight lights up a student's eyes like twin lasers, and you know they have grown beyond the need for your instruction because they have begun to connect for themselves the life of the mind with the life of faith. They have entered the path of faith seeking understanding, a path traveled by earnest seekers in all of humanity's religious Ways. They are now wrestlers with God. During such moments I whisper to myself, "Welcome to the journey, kiddo. But stay alert, because it will be a long bumpy road with your hip thrown out of joint."

The light in Alyssa's[2] eyes was the only bright thing on that Pacific Northwest afternoon. I was watching rain falling hard from slate colored clouds that shrouded the tops of Douglas firs and dimpled pools of water beginning to flood the street that runs outside my office window. Like Herman Melville's Ishmael, I was experiencing a "dark November of the Soul." The way I handled Alyssa's question earlier that morning just didn't satisfy either of us.

The topic of our morning class had been John Hick's "pluralistic hypothesis" and his thesis that Christian theology of religions needs to pass beyond the "Ptolemaic" perspectives of "exclusivist" and "inclusivist" understandings of the world's religious traditions and undergo a "Copernican" paradigm shift to a pluralist theology of religions[3]—not a discussion designed to gather positive teaching evaluations from eighteen-to-twenty-two-year-old undergraduates sitting in a cold classroom at eight o'clock on a wet November morning.

The light in Alyssa's eyes was sparked by my answers to a series of questions that occurred to her after reflecting on Hick's pluralist hypothesis in *An Interpretation of Religion* in conjunction with my views on religious pluralism that she had read in my book, *Wrestling With the Ox*, which was *not* a required text for this particular assignment.

She was frustrated by both books. "I just don't get it, Dr. Ingram. If there's a single Ultimate Reality called God in some religions and something else in other religions, I still don't understand why there are there so many *different* religions? Why isn't there just one religion for everyone? Do you really agree with Hick that no two religions are exactly alike even though there are family resemblances? Do you really think all religious traditions are true for the people who seriously practice them?"

"Yes," I answered, "but that doesn't mean all religious experiences correspond equally to reality, or have equal validity. Marx was half right. Any religion can become an opiate that dulls the mind and emotions. But he was also half wrong. Remember what you read in Frederick Streng's book: religious traditions have more often than not been means of ultimate transformation for religious persons no matter where you find them.[4] There are always historical and cultural issues; everything has to be seen in its own particular context."

"But do you really agree with Hick and Streng?" she demanded.

"Yes, but our conclusions are not identical. There's always more than one way to skin a religious tradition."

"Why?"

"Because I'm a monotheist. Monotheism means there exists one God who creates everything. That includes the world's religions."

My answer came with little reflection, unplanned and spontaneous, blurted like an answer to a Zen koan, because that is exactly what Alyssa's question was. My response wasn't nuanced. Alyssa knew it as well as I. But somehow, it rang true for me as well as for her, if I am a judge of gleams in students' eyes. So she showed up in my office to reflect with me about the implications of monotheism for theological reflection about the realities of religious pluralism—just as I did forty years ago when my eyes were lit up by what my first instructor in history of religions had said about religious pluralism. Her newly found koan had always been mine.

Three months after my initial conversation with Alyssa, I again encountered our koan and another monotheistic response in a paragraph of a recently published book by John Berthrong entitled *The Divine Deli*:

> I not only accept the fact of religious pluralism, namely that god really did create all of the different religions with their fabulous diversity, but that, like all of creation, diversity is fundamentally good. However, this primordial fact of goodness does not mean that there are no problems with the world. All one has to do is look around to make the informed guess that not all is in line with the desire of a loving God. [5]

My conversation with Alyssa and bumping into Berthrong's book now seem like evidence of grace, which as a Lutheran I have come to think operates everywhere in the universe at all times and in all places. Inspired by the gleam in Alyssa's eyes and Berthrong's understanding of monotheism, I shall add my voice to defending the idea that monotheism filtered through the lens of a pluralistic theology of religions reveals the most adequate answer to Alyssa's koan: "Why are there so many religions?" The answer is: "Because there exists a God who created, and continues creating, a universe of wondrous diversity that can be rationally understood." Lurking beneath this claim are epistemological assumptions that require clarification.

Paul Knitter thinks Christian experience of God as incarnated in the historical Jesus is one of the main pushes toward a pluralistic theology of religions. This push, he writes, "comes from two essential characteristics of the Christian God: mysterious and trinitarian."[6] To which I would add a third push: historical consciousness that relativizes all knowledge.[7] Our knowledge of anything, including knowledge of God, is limited by the cultural and historical points of view we occupy at the moment we claim to know anything. If this is true, historical consciousness also teaches us that the reality of God, which Christians apprehend incarnated in the historical Jesus as the Christ of faith, is not limited by what Christians apprehend. In agreement with Knitter, while historical consciousness tells us that every glimpse of truth we can have is intrinsically finite and conditioned, "religious consciousness"—religious experience contextualized by the historicity of all knowledge—tells us that God is more than any human being can grasp.

Consequently, Christian religious experience—which must take place within historical contexts if it is to take place at all—has paradoxical edges: any particular historical encounter with God is as mysterious as it is real, as ambiguous as it is reliable. Mystics and non-mystic theologians who have sensed and urged this recognition of God as utter mystery populate the history of Christian tradition: St. Paul, Augustine, Thomas Aquinas, Julian of Norwich, Meister Eckhart, Martin Luther, John Calvin, John Wesley, and most recently, Karl Rahner, Edward Schillebeekx, Thomas Merton, Paul Tillich, Karl Rahner, Daniel Day Williams, Paul Knitter, and John Cobb.

A paradox that sits at the heart of Christian faith and practice is the incarnation: in the life, death, and resurrection of a particular human life two thousand years ago in a backwater region of the Roman Empire, humanity encountered God within the realities of historical existence. No question. Or in the words of Luther's *Small Catechism*, "This is most certainly true." But while the historical Jesus reveals God, the incarnation does not reveal all that God is. I suspect that most Christian talk of the incarnation as "God in human form" or the "fullness" of the divine mystery in the historical Jesus or the Christian right's unqualified assertion that "Jesus is God" tends to violate the meaning of the incarnation more than preserve it. Affirming the incarnation does not mean that the historical Jesus took on all that constitutes God or that God took on all that constitutes being human—our finitude and limitations. So if the historical Jesus, as the Second *persona* of the Trinity, defines *who* God is for Christians, the historical Jesus does not exhaust *what* God is. To ignore the limitations of the incarnation is to fall into docetism—the heresy that stresses the divinity of Jesus as it denatures his humanity. Much evangelical and fundamentalist Christian theology is docetic.

Consequently, perceiving God's incarnation in the historical Jesus is simultaneously recognizing that God cannot be limited to the historical Jesus. The reality Christians encounter in Jesus is truly available and found beyond Jesus. Or in the words of Edward Schillebeeckx:

> The revelation of God in Jesus, as the Christian gospel proclaims, does not mean that God absolutizes a historical particularity (be it even in Jesus of Nazareth). From that revelation in Jesus we learn that no single historical particularity can be called absolute and that therefore, because of the relativity present in Jesus, every person can encounter God outside of Jesus, especially in our worldly history and in the many religions that have arisen form it.[8]

No particular religious tradition, therefore, has the final or the exclusive or the inclusive Word about God. Final words limit and demystify God and are more useful for the politics of power in Church hierarchies than relevant to the religious needs of faithful Christians. Final words are, as Wilfred Cantwell Smith never tired of pointing out, forms of idolatry—*shirk* in Islamic formulation, meaning reducing God to that which is not God and surrendering to it.[9] An idol is not something that mediates God to faithful persons, but something that seeks to confine God to a series of theological propositions or a liturgical system or a particular book or a particular institution claimed to be the final mediator of God. Most idols occur in our individual and collective heads.

When one reflects carefully about it, the reality Christians name "God" cannot be confined to any one religious tradition because the reality of God—that which constitutes God as God—is both unity and plurality. I agree with Knitter that this is the deepest content of Christian experience symbolized by the doctrine of the trinity:[10] God is one and God is plural, which, as it turns out, can be conceptualized in the categories of process theology. God's "primordial nature," meaning God's self-identity through the moments of God's time, is what God always is as God, beyond the categories of thought and always in interdependent relationship with the universe God created and continually sustains as the First Person of the Trinity (the "Father").[11] Yet the primordial nature of God is always in non-dual interdependency with the "plurality" of God's "consequent nature"—God as God mutually affects and is affected by all things and events in the universe throughout the moments of God's experience—two thousand years ago through the Second Person (the Son) and before and after the death of Jesus through the Third Person (the Holy Spirit). God in God's primordial nature needs "manyness" to be God in God's consequent nature.

The point is not that God has one nature inadequately expressed in different religious traditions, although this seems to me to be true. The point is that there are real and genuine differences within what medieval Christian mystics called "the Godhead" and what process theology calls God's primordial nature and God's continuous interaction with the universe and the great variety of human communities that constitute God's consequent nature. As Alfred North Whitehead noted, since God cannot be an exception to the metaphysical principles through which God creates the universe, plurality seems essential to reality—"the way things really are"—from subatomic particles to religious traditions to God. Metaphysically, the principle of interdependence is at the heart of existence. Accordingly, just as God cannot be reduced to a unity that would remove the differences between the three persons of the Trinity, so Christians can trust that the plurality of the world's religions cannot be reduced to the kind of unity that would remove the real differences among the various traditions in order to prove the superiority of one and the inferiority of the rest.

Emboldened by the practice of Buddhist-Christian dialogue and John Keenan's "Mahayana reading" of the Gospel of Mark,[12] if I were to preach a sermon that incorporated the pluralistic principles I have thus far outlined, I would focus on two texts from the Gospel of Mark. First, Mark 9:33-37:

And they came to Capernaum; and when he was in the house he asked them, "What were you discussing on the way?" But they were silent; for on the way they had discussed with one another who was the greatest. And he sat down and called the twelve; and he said to them, "If any one would be first, he must be last of all and servant of all." And he took a child, and put him in the midst of them; and taking him in his arms, he said to them," Whoever receives one such child in my name receives me; and whoever receives me, receives not me, but him who sent me.

Jesus' question to Peter, "Who do you say that I am?" is the heart of Christian self-understanding. The question must be answered differently in every age. We do not live in the first century or the middle ages or the nineteenth century. Clinging to past images of Jesus and his relation to God simply will not do in a contemporary context of global religious and cultural pluralism. Not surprising, since Christians have been practicing faith within globally pluralistic contexts for two thousand years.

Yet we still haven't got it right, even though the answer to Jesus' question to Peter is right in front of us, as it was for the disciples, stalking us and Peter like a cougar after prey. According to Mark's gospel, the disciples didn't get it right either, even though they followed Jesus around Palestine for perhaps a year. Jesus tried to tell them, yet even they didn't understand what they had heard until after Jesus was killed.

The scene is this. Jesus and the disciples have returned to Capernaum after an extended journey. On the way to Caesarea Philippi Jesus had questioned the disciples about his identity. Now on the way back to Capernaum, the disciples are arguing about their own self-images. When Jesus questions them they fall silent with embarrassment because they have been arguing about the preeminence of self—over who is the greatest. They are like fundamentalists everywhere in all religious traditions—trapped in the conventional categories of their ideologies. They, like Jesus, are practicing Jews. But unlike Jesus, they cling to their culture's conventional Judaism so tightly they can't hear the music behind the lyrics of either Jewish practices or Jesus' teachings. Like legalists and fundamentalists everywhere, their path is one of fabricating verbal argumentation, of imaging a self—or a particular community of selves—exalted above others at the center of their conventional universe. Their trip with Jesus has not awakened them. Instead, they see Jesus as their ticket to glory.

21

So once more Jesus instructs them about discipleship. His method is to subvert their notions of discipleship. Discipleship has nothing to do with preeminence. "He who would be first must be last," he says. To make one's self last means negating the absolute nature of one's ego-self. This is why receiving Jesus and the one who sent him in Mark and elsewhere in other Gospel texts is described as the receiving of a little child—of one who has not yet developed a strong self-image, of one who has no rank or particular importance. It is Jesus who approaches the disciples and the readers of Mark as a child, with no rank or importance whatsoever. It is God who sent Jesus, who approaches the disciples and us as a child, not as the romanticized image of sweet innocence, but the weakest of the weak.

Our first response as readers of Mark's text is to disassociate ourselves from the disciples. In previous verses Jesus had just been speaking about the inevitability of his suffering and death. So the disciples' insensitivity to Jesus' fate, combined with their crass egoism, is not a stance a reader is likely to want to embrace. But by a rhetorical slight of hand, the Markan Jesus directly addresses the reader—meaning us—through a series of paradoxical "if" and "whoever" statements: "If anyone would be first, he must be last of all and servant of all"; "Whoever receives one such child in my name receives me"; "Whoever receives me, receives not me but him who sent me." In other words, anyone who would practice the Way of Jesus must reverse the pattern of imagined expectations and conventional understanding of religious traditions and plunge into the paradoxical world of Jesus' "doubling-back" discourse, and therein enter into the kingdom of nobodies that is the Kingdom of God.

The experience of paradox is the experience of being bracketed between seemingly incompatible but nevertheless coexisting pairs of opposites. Even Mark's language about God is paradoxical. Who is the "who" that sent Jesus? Why does Mark not explicitly identify God as Jesus' sender. The Markan Jesus simply says that to receive the weakest of the weak is to receive him and "him who sent me." In the same way, the voice of God speaks from the heavens at Jesus' baptism in chapter 1:1, and again from the cloud at Jesus' transfiguration. Yet Mark fails to mention just whose voice is speaking. And again, when the Markan Jesus addresses God in Gethsemani, no voice is heard at all. But Jesus is the son of God and our assumption that the voices Mark allows us to hear are from God is not mistaken. What *is* mistaken is that we know what this means. Not only is Jesus impossible to identify in clear definitions, God is too. What then could it mean to be great?

Now from Mark 9:38-40:

> John said to him, "Teacher, we saw a man casting out demons in your name, and we forbade him, because he was not following us." But Jesus said, "Do not forbid him; for no one who does a mighty work in my name will be able soon after to speak evil of me. For he who is not against us is for us."

Now the disciple John changes the question by clinging to the name of Jesus to bring up the issue of who belongs to the Jesus movement. After all, throughout Mark's gospel, Jesus harshly criticizes various groups of people—Pharisees, scribes, temple priests. Who could blame John for concluding that the disciples constitute a well-defined exclusive group over and against outsiders. Indeed, defining a social identity was an important issue for the early church. It still is. But party spirit does not come from receiving Jesus and God as one would receive a child, but from a fearful mind that draws artificial boundaries around people as a religious prophylaxis to protect the community from coming into contact with whatever it regards as threatening.

Like Paul, Jesus does not recommend party identity, but opens up community to anyone who is not against him. There are no fixed criteria for membership in the Jesus community—beyond the requirement that one not be against it. Mark's Jesus does not define Christian self-identity. Jesus' teachings in Mark are inclusive, not exclusive: they apply to all who are not against Jesus, not only Christians, but also non-Christians: Buddhists who revere Jesus as an awakened person, that is, a Bodhisattva; Muslims who revere Jesus as one of the greatest prophets; Jews who see Jesus as a reformer calling people to a renewed practice of the Torah; Hindus who see Jesus as one of many incarnations of Brahman.

Of course, these non-Christians do not accept Christian *ideas* about Jesus. Yet Jesus' teaching recorded here in Mark asserts no such requirement. To be *for* Jesus does not necessarily mean to accept ideas *about* Jesus. Ideas about Jesus—creeds, doctrines, theological constructions in general—flow out of conventional wisdom and are tied to historical and cultural contexts and thereby are empty of unchanging essence and once-and-for-all timeless meanings. His Jesus and the God who sent Jesus shy away from self-definition. The Messiah is not anything like the disciples' triumphalist expectations, but one who experiences the sufferings and sorrows and joys of a lived life. The follower of Jesus is not one who belongs to the proper group. Anyone who is not against Jesus is a follower of Jesus.

So what does Mark teach us about following the way of Jesus two thousand years after the disciples tried and failed? I think Mark teaches negative and positive lessons.

Negatively, Mark's deconstruction of human pretensions about who is greatest, along with claims that any single group of followers of Jesus has an exclusive claim on Jesus and the one who sent Jesus, tells us that Christian faith is not about ripping biblical texts out of context as a means of proving who's really Christian and who's not. Mark teaches us that no human being and no religious community is greater than another human being or religious community. Mark teaches us that faith is not adherence to a set of doctrinal propositions about Jesus and the one who sent Jesus. Mark teaches us that Jesus and the one who sent him cannot be constrained by ritual and theological systems. Mark teaches us that clinging to conventional practices and conventional understandings that try to lock God within the safe boundaries of our cultural expectations while excluding those who do not see things our way is not faith, but unfaith. Mark teaches us that we should never reduce faith to belief in a set of doctrinal propositions, that we should never confuse theological reflection, which is faith seeking understanding, with ideology.

Positively, Mark teaches us that we find Jesus and the one who sent Jesus incarnated in the ordinary, in loving relationships between people, in struggle against economic, political, gender, and racial injustice, in struggle for ecological justice that frees nature—God's creation—from human exploitation. Following the way of Jesus is not a matter of membership in a particular Christian group or wearing a particular Christian label like "Lutheran" or "Roman Catholic" or "Presbyterian" or "Baptist." The Jesus community that Mark envisions includes anyone who is not against Jesus: the socially engaged Buddhist layman Sulak Sivaraksa, who has time and again placed his life in danger for his criticism of the Thai government's financial involvement in the drug trade and sex trade of his country; Dr. Cecil Murray, senior pastor of the First AME Church in Los Angeles, whose educational vision and social outreach to the poor and economically oppressed has become a model for similar social programs throughout the counties of Southern California; Mahatma Gandhi, who followed the principle of non-violence in his struggle to free his people from British colonial oppression; Gandhi's Muslim friend, Badhsha Khan, who transformed the Qur'an's teaching of *jihad* or "holy war" into Islamic non-violent resistance against the injustice of British colonialism; Martin Luther King Jr. who apprehended Jesus and the one who sent Jesus in his fight against American racism.

All of these are followers of Jesus, as are each of us, when we feed the poor; when we refuse to oppress people because of gender, ethnicity, or race; when we do not confuse membership in the Jesus community with membership in any particular form of the institutional church. We are followers of Jesus when we renounce the idolatry of no-salvation-outside-the-church-or-explicit-Christian-belief-exclusivism. We are followers of Jesus and the one who sent Jesus when we refuse to destroy nature through unbridled consumerism. We find Jesus and the one who sent Jesus incarnated in the Kingdom of God that is the Kingdom of Nobodies.

Of course, the way I have sermonically interpreted the historicity of all ideas and the Trinity through the lenses of process theology is not the only possible interpretation of the Trinity or of Mark's Gospel. But there are other Buddhist and Christian sources that lead to similar conclusions. One of the most important is Buddhist experience of awakened compassion (*karuṇā*) and Christian experience that God is unbounded love. Comprehending what Buddhists mean by compassionate wisdom can deepen Christian understanding of God's character as unbounded love.

In Buddhist meditative experience, "compassion" is the experience of empathy for the suffering and joys of all living things—all sentient beings—that accompanies the wisdom that reveals all things and events as mutually interrelated and interdependent. With the wisdom that accompanies Awakening, an Awakened One disinterestedly, meaning "dispassionately," experiences the suffering of all beings as his or her own, because in a universe of interdependence, that's exactly what they are. Consequently, awakened compassion engenders what Thich Nhat Hanh calls "social engagement"—engagement with the suffering of all sentient beings to relieve them of suffering. Thus, like a skillful and dispassionate physician confronted with universal suffering, an Awakened One seeks to relieve all beings of suffering while not letting the suffering "get to him."

In Buddhist thought (and in current English usage), "disinterest" does not mean "non-interest," but "non-attachment." Yet, unlike the disinterested character of Buddhist wise compassion, love in Christian tradition is passionate care for the well-being of all living beings living in a world "God so loved." In Christian experience, God's character is unbounded love interdependent with justice because God gives preference to, that is, God is attached to, the poor and the oppressed. As Christians, we are called to passionately love one another and all things in the universe as God passionately loves us and all things in the universe. Or to paraphrase the thirteenth-century Beguine mystic, Marguerite Porete, we should seek to be so unified with God that we experience the universe as God experiences the universe and love it accordingly.[13]

I have argued elsewhere that passionate love and disinterested compassionate wisdom are non-dual, meaning they are neither identical nor separate, but are what they are in interdependent relation to the other, like "heads and tails" are two interdependent sides of the same coin. Neither love nor disinterested compassionate wisdom, like heads and tails, has meaning or existence apart from the other.[14] The disinterested character of compassionate wisdom and the passionate character of unconditional love can be appropriated by Christians. In Buddhist teaching, wisdom arises through the practice of meditation and is doctrinally characterized as experiential awareness of the utter interdependency of all things and events in every moment of space-time. In other words, all particular things and events are constituted by their ongoing relationships with all things and events in the universe at that moment. Buddhist doctrine describes this process as *pratītya-samutpāda* or "dependent co-arising." A central content of Awakened wisdom is experiential confirmation of the truth of the doctrine of "dependent co-arising."

Buddhist texts describe this experience as "beyond language," or in the words of Zen tradition, "beyond words and letters." But symbolic images can give clues to those of us who are not Awakened that help us imagine what such wisdom is like—as long as one does not cling to symbolic images. One such clue is the Hua-yen Buddhist simile of Indra's net. In the heavenly abode of the Hindu deity, Indra, there is hung a wonderful net that stretches out in all directions. The net's weaver has strung a single jewel in each eye, and since the net is infinite is all directions, the jewels are infinite in number. If we look closely at a single jewel, we see that its polished surface reflects every other jewel. Not only this, each jewel reflected in the one we are looking at simultaneously reflects all the other jewels, so that there occurs an infinitely reflecting process. Thus, like the jewels of Indra's net, the universe is a vast body made up of an infinity of individuals all creating and sustaining each other. That is, the universe is a self-creating, self-sustaining, and self-defining organism. Hua-yen Buddhism calls this universe *dharma-dhatu*, which Francis Cook translates as a "cosmos" or "universe" of "organic mutual identity and interdependence."[15]

Accordingly, interdependence means that no thing or event is separate from another thing and event. Every thing and event is implicated in all things and events; all things and events are ingredients in a single thing and event. It is experiential awareness of universal interdependence, which is central to what Buddhists mean by awakened wisdom, that generates a mind of awakened compassion. For in an interdependent universe, the suffering of a single being is the suffering of all beings. If there is even one single being that is not awakened, no one is fully awakened. We are all in this universe together. Realizing this, an Awakened One, in Mahayana Buddhist language, a Bodhisattva, is moved to work for the release of all sentient beings from suffering because an Awakened One has realized that the suffering of other sentient beings is also his or her own. Accordingly, in Buddhist experience, compassion arises from the wisdom that reveals the metaphysical structure of reality as interdependent. Interdependence is neither "good" nor "bad" but simply "is." Since all things and events are interconnected, the appropriate response is interacting with all things and events with dispassionate disinterest, which is never non-interest.

As wise compassion is modeled for Buddhists by the historical Gautama, so God's character as unconditioned love is modeled for Christians by the historical Jesus. Christians are called to unconditionally love all human beings and the creatures of God's creation as God unconditionally loves all human beings and the creatures of God's creation, with no ego strings attached. Such love is not detached, but passionately involved. We are all brothers and sisters because the existence of all creation originates from

27

God. We should therefore relate to one another according to what is needed, which may often be different from what is wanted. In this sense, love is "non-personal": like rain falling on the earth, God's love falls on all without regard to social status, economic influence, or merit, so don't take it personally. Yet the interdependent flip side of unconditional love is justice, which in the prophetic tradition out of which Jesus lived and taught, is liberation from all institutional and personal obstacles that cause suffering and prevent persons from achieving what they need for meaningful life in community with one another, with nature, and with God. Love as the struggle for justice for all persons as well for all other sentient beings is involved and passionate.

Christian practice of unconditional love can gain much through appropriating Buddhist experience of compassionate wisdom. The context for unconditional love is the interdependent structure of reality itself. Christians need to awaken, that is, "wise up" to this structure in order to understand that there is no "other" dualistically separated from oneself. Every thing and event is mutually co-created by the plurality of God's universe. We are this plurality looking at and thinking about itself. Such wisdom expresses itself as compassion: the apprehension that the suffering and needs of others, particularly for justice, is our suffering and need for justice. Grounded by compassionate wisdom, unbounded love is active struggle for justice and release from suffering for all creatures within the rough-and-tumble of historical existence. In this sense, the practice of unbounded love requires guidance by compassionate wisdom.

Thus, for Christians, love of God that is the first commandment engenders the second commandment: unbounded love directed by compassionate wisdom takes priority over all other ethical injunctions, religious practices, theological systems, and institutional demands. The second commandment means loving one's neighbor and has priority over proclaiming doctrine or formally worshipping God. The New Testament standard is this: first work out things with your neighbor, brother or sister, then go to church or synagogue or mosque or temple (Matt 5:23-24). Don't allow religious practice, with its professions of doctrines and ritual observances, to get in the way of doing good for your neighbor. It's better to break the Sabbath than to fail in loving your neighbor (Matt 12:12). Viewed from the role loving compassionate wisdom played in the faith and

28

practice of Jesus, there is something fundamentally wrong with traditional Christian views of other religions.

For starters, to practice loving compassionate wisdom means engaging non-Christians in dialogue, not as "other," but as persons who in mutual interdependence with us seek truth. In dialogue we listen to our non-Christian brothers and sisters with real openness to what they are saying. Dialogue means treating them as we would want them to treat us. It means listening to their witness to truth as we would want them to listen to ours. It means confronting them when we think they are wrong, even as we must be ready to be confronted by them when they think we are wrong. In short, to love one's neighbors wisely and compassionately means to be in dialogue with them.

However, traditional Christian attitudes toward the world's religions—both the inclusive and exclusive models—are obstacles to treating neighbors with love in dialogue. An exclusive model interprets all religious traditions different from one's own as false. Persons participating in these "other" traditions are in error and in need of conversion to one's own tradition. An inclusive model asserts that whatever truth exists in a religious tradition other than one's own is a partial reflection of the full truth of one's own religious way.[16] Persons participating in these traditions are not in complete error, but need conversions to one's own tradition to be in full contact with saving truth. Both models are in conflict with the practice of loving compassionate wisdom.

For me, as a Christian monotheist, the questions are these: can we respect our non-Christian brothers and sisters and be open to them if we must believe before we even meet them that our truth is better than theirs, that they are inferior to us in what they hold to be true and sacred? And can we affirm and love them when we are convinced with *a priori* certainty that they will have to agree with our truth if they are going to arrive at the fullness of God's truth? Whenever we hold up a truth claim and insist that according to the will of God it is the only or the absolutely final norm in which all other truths have to be included, then we cannot treat them as our brothers and sisters in God. While absolutizing Christian tradition into a universal norm for measuring all religious claims does enable us to *confront* non-Christians as "other," it does not allow us to *encounter* them or *be encountered* by them as brothers and sisters as loving compassionate wisdom requires.

Along with Paul Knitter, I think there is growing awareness among many Christians—both in the pews of churches and among theologians—of a discrepancy between theological reflection and ethical practice. This discrepancy lies between the view of non-Christian traditions asserted by traditional exclusive and inclusive Christian belief and teaching and the conduct toward non-Christian persons required by Christian ethics—an ethics that can only be based on loving compassionate wisdom if it is Christian.

Essentially, the conflict many Christians experience is between theological orthodoxy—right beliefs—and orthopraxy—right behavior.[17] Partly this has to do with the fact that as more Christians have come to know non-Christians, it has become clear that our non-Christian brothers and sisters are in general neither less nor more kind, thoughtful, loving, wise, or compassionate than are Christians.[18] Increasingly, Christians are experiencing tension, if not contradiction, between the first and second commandments and the final commandment of their Christian faith—to spread the Gospel to all nations as they extend love to all human beings and the creatures of the Earth with compassionate wisdom. While Jesus instructed his disciples to love their neighbors as themselves, he is also said to have given them a final instruction—to go forth into the world and make his message known to all human beings. Christians are called upon to love their neighbors and to make the good news about Jesus known so as to make disciples of all human beings.

Again in Luther's language, "This is most certainly true." Yet for whatever reason, throughout Christian history Christians have tended to make the final commandment more important than the first and second commandments. Christians have spread the Gospel throughout the world, but have all too often not loved their non-Christian brothers and sisters wisely or compassionately in the process. Given the inclusive and exclusive models for understanding our third commandment, Christians have frequently not respected, listened to, learned from, or affirmed their non-Christian neighbors as loving compassionate wisdom requires.

The theological and ethical contradiction between the first and second commandments and the last commandment, between Christian ethical *praxis* and Christian doctrine, between orthopraxy and orthodoxy has a long history. However, given the priority of the orthopraxy of loving one's neighbor as oneself wisely and compassionately over the orthodoxy of theological doctrine—as modeled by Mark's account of the historical Jesus—exclusive and inclusive models for understanding our final commission should be rejected and replaced by the practice of interreligious dialogue guided by loving compassionate wisdom. It's not that theological reflection is unimportant. Theology is, after all, faith seeking understanding. But doctrinal orthodoxy is not more important that the practice of unbounded love and compassionate wisdom. Like everything else in the universe, the practice of loving compassionate wisdom and theological reflection are interdependent.

Forty years ago, when I was Alyssa's age and had first encountered our *koan*—"If there is one God, why are there so many religions?"—I decided I could either reason my way into or out of Christian tradition. I was a young undergraduate philosophy major then who often confused "love of wisdom" for ideology. So I decided to "explore the world's religions," a passion that to this day turns me on like a switch intellectually and spiritually. As an historian of religions, I have witnessed great creativity and great stupidity among representatives of all the religious traditions I have studied. Still it's the creative persons who always stand out—faithful Christians, Buddhists, Muslims, Hindus, Jews, Native Americans—living integrated and creative lives within the conditions of historical existence. Such men and women teach me that no single religious tradition can make claims to be the final repository of truth. To me, this is the main empirical evidence that falsifies the theological imperialism of universal truth claims, both Christian and non-Christian.

So when it comes down to it, I now suspect that in the end, one's faith is a matter of being, in one way or another, like St. Paul, "struck from one's horse." I think that's true whether one is a Christian or a Buddhist or a Muslim or a Hindu or a Jew. For It all depends on what or who "speaks" to you. I admire Mahatma Gandhi. I admire Mohammed and the Buddha and the Jewish sages. The Sufi poets and the Hindu epics make my heart sing. The socially engaged Buddhist faith of Sulak Sivraksa, Dr. A. T. Ariyaratne, and the Dalai Lama reveal to me the lack of depth in my own Christian faith. I admire these people, but I don't "experience" them. They don't "speak" to me.

I don't mean that Jesus talks to me. Whenever I listen to fundamentalist Christians describe Jesus as a kind of best buddy, I feel a little creepy. In the Gospel of John, Jesus is reported to have said: "I live in you and you live in me." For me, this is sufficient. A Christian is someone who "gets" that and spends the rest of his or her life trying to figure what it all means—a Christian form of wrestling with God. You find yourself in a state of faith, that is, you "get" it—whether one is a Christian or a Buddhist or a Muslim or a Jew or a Hindu—the way you catch a cold, by contagion. Sometimes, the experience is like being knocked off a horse. So reason and argument, it seems to me, do not engender faith, although they may express faith. No religious faith is reducible to "belief" in doctrines and propositions.

A few years ago I asked a friend who is a Lutheran pastor, Dan Erlander, what he thought about Jesus' relation to God. "Jesus is someone who had access, in the most compassionate way, to what being human is really like," he answered. "In some sense, God was 'in' Jesus because only God can do that."

In the church's sacraments, Dan finds an understanding that there's a descending force—like rain on a hot August day in the Pacific Northwest—that he identifies as the Holy Spirit. Through his work with university students as a campus pastor, his ministry to the homeless, and his leadership in dealing with local ecological issues, Dan has come to think that the resurrection "somehow involved Jesus doing something with the way the universe works." Then he talked about an experience he has every time he celebrates the Eucharist. It always happens when his congregation gets to the point in the liturgy when everyone sings, "Christ has died, Christ has risen, Christ will come again." "I don't understand that," he said. Then he flashed a broad grin. "But I'm for it."

On the simplest level, then, Christian faith is about trusting that, no matter what human beings have done, are doing, or will do, God makes something new and wonderful from this mess. Life doesn't end on a cross, not because of anything human beings do, but because of what the loving compassionate wisdom at the heart of the universe itself is doing. Of course it would be ridiculously inappropriate to say to someone in terrible grief or pain that everything will be all right. Christian faith is not identical with insensitivity and stupidity. But there is a sense in which "I'm for it."

None of this—absolutely none—requires asserting the superiority of Christianity or the historical Jesus over non-Christian traditions or the historical human beings revered in non-Christian traditions. I'm a monotheist. God's unbounded wise compassionate wisdom is at work in them all in its own distinctively pluralistic way, and "I'm for it."

Alyssa continues to meditate on her *koan*. Our conversation years ago led her to add religious studies as a second major during her undergraduate years at Pacific Lutheran University. From here, her path led her to Luther Seminary in St. Paul, Minnesota. Now married with two children, she lives in deliberate simplicity outside a small, isolated ranching community in North Dakota and spends her professional time as a pastor of a small Lutheran congregation helping them contextualize their Christian faith with the realities of religious pluralism—a pluralism that in her neck of the universe includes the spirituality of the Lakota and Cheyenne people, on behalf of whom she struggles for economic and social justice against some very powerful and wealthy politicians, ranchers, and farmers. On the side she leads a small group of people in contemplative prayer and Zen Buddhist *zazen* ("seated meditation") to deepen her openness to God and to keep her spirit from being eaten alive by her passion for political and social activism. It's one of the ways she wrestles with God that she learned from Thich Nhat Hanh's advice to his students: "Inner work involves outer work."

Alyssa hates television and refuses to own one. But she is a voracious reader, her favorite author at the moment being Annie Dillard. In one of her recent letters she cited this passage from Dillard's *Pilgrim at Tinker Creek* as a description of her wrestling match with God:

> Ezekiel excoriates false prophets as those who have "not gone up into the gaps." The gaps are the thing. The gaps are the spirit's one home, the altitudes and the latitudes so dazzlingly spare and clean that the spirit can discover itself for the first time like a once-blind man unbound. The gaps are the cliffs in the rock where you cower to see the back parts of God; they are the fissures between mountains and cells the wind lances through, the icy narrowing fiords splitting the cliffs of mystery. Go up into the gaps. If you can find them; they shift and vanish too. Stalk the gaps. Squeak into a gap in the soil, turn and unlock—more

than a maple—a universe. This is how you spend this afternoon, and tomorrow morning, and tomorrow afternoon. *Spend* the afternoon. You can't take it with you.[19]

ENDNOTES

[1] Loren Eisley, "The Hidden Teacher," *The Unexpected Universe* (New York: Harcourt, 1969) 48–66.

[2] Of course, this is not her real name since I wish to protect the confidentiality of our conversation, at her request.

[3] John Hick, *An Interpretation of Religion: Human Responses to the Transcendent* (New Haven: Yale University Press, 1989) chapter 14.

[4] Frederick J. Streng, *Understanding Religious Life* (Belmont, Calif.: Wadsworth, 1985) chapter 1.

[5] John H. Berthrong, *The Divine Deli: Religious Identity in the North American Cultural Mosaic* (Maryknoll, N.Y.: Orbis, 1999).

[6] Paul F. Knitter, *Jesus and the Other Names* (Maryknoll, N.Y.: Orbis, 1996) 37.

[7] See Van A. Harvey, *The Historian and the Believer* (Philadelphia: Westminster, 1966) chapters 3–8.

[8] Edward Schillebeeckx, *The Church: The Human Story of God*, trans. John Bowden (New York: Crossroad, 1990) 184, also cited in Knitter, *Jesus and the Other Names*, 38.

[9] Wilfred Cantwell Smith, *Faith and Belief* (Princeton, N.J.: Princeton University Press, 1979) chapter 3.

[10] Knitter, *Jesus and the Other Names*, 38–39.

[11] "Father" is in parentheses because while this is traditional Christian usage, it is troublesome because of its sexist overtones. "Father" is an inadequate designation of God as the creator and sustainer of the universe. One could use "Mother" or both, depending on what one wished to stress theologically, and both would adequately, but incompletely, point to Christian experience of God. In my own theological reflection, I sometimes think of God as Mother, sometimes as Father, sometimes as both—Mother and Father. For a concise description of this aspect of Trinitarian theology, see John B. Cobb Jr., *Christ In A Pluralistic Age* (Philadelphia: Westminster, 1975) 259–64.

[12] John P. Keenan, *The Gospel of Mark: A Mahayana Reading* (Maryknoll, N.Y.: Orbis, 1995) 224–28. I have carefully followed Keenan's commentary on these texts, with gratitude.

[13] Maguerite Porete, *The Mirror of Simple Souls*, trans. and introduced by Ellen L. Babinsky (New York: Paulist, 1993) 189–93.

[14] See my *Wrestling with the Ox*, 126–31.

[15] Francis H. Cook, "The Jewel Net of Indra," in *Nature in Asian Traditions of Thought*, ed. J. Baird Callicott and Roger T. Ames (Albany, N.Y.: SUNY Press, 1989) 215.

[16] For an analysis of several versions of theological exclusivism and inclusivism, see my, *Wrestling with the Ox*, chapter 1.

[17] Knitter, *Jesus and the Other Names*, 40–45.

[18] In this regard, my experience is similar to Hick's. "My own inevitably limited experience . . . . has led me to think that the spiritual and moral fruits of these faiths, although different, are more or less on a par with the fruits of Christianity; and reading some of the literature of the different traditions, both some of their scriptures and philosophies and also some of their novels and poetry portraying ordinary life, has reinforced this impression." John Hick, *A Christian Theology of Religions* (Louisville: Westminster John Knox, 1995) 12–16.

[19] Annie Dillard, *Pilgrim at Tinker Creek* (New York: Harper and Row, 1974) 268–69.

Chapter 3

On the Practice of Faith:
A Lutheran's Interior Dialogue with Buddhism

I earn my living practicing the craft of history of religions. It's one of the ways I wrestle with God. In Lutheran theological language, this is my "calling" and "vocation." I know this to be true because of how I was first opened to an amazing world of religious pluralism over forty years ago during my first undergraduate history of religions course. I am still amazed by this world. The history of religions continues to inform my self-understanding and has recently become for me a primary mode of theological reflection and practice that intensely energizes both my exterior conceptual dialogue with Buddhist doctrine and teaching and my interior dialogue with Buddhist meditative practice.[1]

So my vocation is teaching an academic field of inquiry I love to young people as I engage in research and writing. I am paid for doing this by a university related to the Evangelical Lutheran Church in America that bills itself as a "new American university" located in one of the most culturally pluralistic and beautiful regions in the United States. While I'm not sure what a "New American University" actually is, I am convinced that my professional life constitutes for me some of the evidence of the grace that Christian tradition in general—and Luther's theology in

36

particular—describe as flowing "in, with, and under" this universe like a waterfall, or over it like a tidal wave.

Admittedly, all this is highly confessional, perhaps too confessional, for an academic scholar reflecting on how Buddhist traditions of practice have informed his Christian practice. Yet when it comes down to it, all theological reflection—as well as the discipline of practice itself—is confessional. We can only write about our interior journey as this is informed by the particular community of faith that gives context to our practice, for it is not probable that most persons can be religious in general, but only in particular.[2] After all, as I have noted, Carmelite nuns do not ordinarily seek or experience non-duality with the Buddha Nature, nor do Zen Buddhist nuns ordinarily seek or experience interior union with Christ the Bridegroom. Yet sometimes, a few historians of religions and a few Christian theologians and Buddhist philosophers are able to participate in communities of faith and practice other than their own. This too seems to me a sign of grace.

I have learned two lessons from interior dialogue with Buddhists as this shakes out in my particular practice. First, our interior journeys lead us through time—forward and back, seldom in a straight line, most often in spirals. Each of us is moving and changing in relationship to others and to the world, and, if one is grasped by Christian faith, to God, or if grasped by Buddhist faith (*śraddha*), the Dharma.[3] As we discover what our interior journeys teach us, we remember; remembering, we discover; and most intensely do we discover when our separate journeys converge. It is at spots of Christian and Buddhist convergence that I have experienced the most dramatic and creatively transformative processes of interreligious dialogue.

Second, as a Lutheran it strikes me as a bit glib to suggest that the focus of practice is "God" or, if Buddhist, "Awakening," because I often feel intellectually and emotionally blindsided by what people who practice mean by these words. The question, always an epistemological one, is what do these terms mean as we practice whatever we practice? Plenty of theological-philosophical propositions can be strung together to answer this question, and, I think, it is important to guide practice by theological-philosophical reflection. But we must never cling to belief in propositions, because the moment we do, they will hide the reality to which they point. Conceptualizing and believing in rational propositions is a necessary beginning because it is a form of "faith seeking understanding." But faith is never, in Christian or Buddhist tradition, identical with belief in propositions. Faith implies being grasped by and betting one's life on, that is, trusting, the reality to which propositions may sometimes point, a grasp that goes beyond propositions, is not caused by propositions, yet cannot be experienced non-propositionally, since even the statement "God" or "Awakening" is beyond the grasp of language, yet is still a "proposition."

Of course, much also depends on the meaning of "practice." The clearest discussion of the meaning of "practice" I have found within the context of Buddhist-Christian dialogue is a remarkable essay written by John C. Maraldo entitled "The Hermeneutics of Practice in Dogen and Francis of Assisi."[4] Maraldo notes that the popular understanding of practice is instrumental: practice (*praxis*) is something different from theory (*theoria*): theory and theoretical knowledge are ends in themselves; practice is an end outside itself.[5] Much discussion of practice within the context of Buddhist-Christian dialogue assumes this popular understanding. For example, one often hears from Zen Buddhists and advocates of Christian "spirituality" that doctrines are meaningless, that the mind should be emptied of such theoretical stuff so that what's *really* real about reality can be experienced directly by a mind unfettered by theoretical constructions. Seen from this perspective, practice is an instrumental means for achieving something we don't think we have. So one practices meditation or contemplative prayer as a method to achieve a "beyond-all-language" experience of awakening or union with God.

Such instrumental understandings that bifurcate practice from achievement of a goal presuppose that we need to do something to achieve whatever it is we don't think we have, as if we were on the outside of our lives looking in. But this does not quite square with Christian contemplative traditions or Buddhist meditative traditions, and it is certainly contrary to Luther's teaching about faith and grace and his rejection of all "works" as instrumental means for creating a redemptive relationship with God. Buddhist tradition, Roman Catholic and Orthodox contemplative tradition, and mainline Protestant tradition agree: we have everything we are ever going to have and there is nothing to gain—absolutely nothing— through practice, because practice and attainment are non-dual.

For me, as a Lutheran Christian, therefore, religious practice is the disciplined performance of faith without regard to achieving goals. If you will, it is a kind of Christian "actionless-action" (Chinese, *wu-wei*), since faith is not something I decide to "have" by any act of the will to believe. One *finds* oneself in a state of faith, one does not *practice* oneself into a state of faith, since there is no time when we or any other thing or event in the universe is ever separated from God—at least according to the Genesis creation story as read through the Prologue of the Gospel of John.

Of course, this presupposes Luther's teaching that grace operates universally at all times and in all places in the universe. For me, this means that if one is engaged in a religious practice, one is drawn to it by grace through faith alone, which means there is nothing to gain by practice that one does not already have. Within Buddhist tradition, Shinran's teaching that even awakening itself is created in us by Amida Buddha's compassionate "other-power" points to a parallel Buddhist understanding of the experience of the utter interdependence of grace, faith, and practice.[6]

Any activity that takes practice to be performed skillfully will do to illustrate what I mean. Recall such activities as practicing a musical instrument or dance, learning a language, practicing a martial art, doing floral arrangement or the tea ceremony, or writing poetry. To practice these activities requires repeated effort and concentrated performance. Such activities are daily disciplines exercised for no other reason than their performance—unless one is a novice who mistakenly interprets practice as different from skilled performance. But as an activity becomes "practiced," and proficient performance is acquired, the gap between what we will and what we do disappears. "It may even be said that during any practice there is no room for desires or intentions which separate our present performance from an imagined ideal, what we are doing from how we wish we were doing it."[7] Consequently, my particular "practice" has evolved into three interdependent forms: (1) theological reflection, (2) centering prayer, and (3) social engagement.

According to my colleague Patricia O'Connell Killen, theological reflection is a discipline that becomes an art by its practice. She defines "theological reflection" as

the discipline of exploring individual and corporate experience in conversation with the wisdom of a religious heritage. The conversation is a genuine dialogue that seeks to hear from our own beliefs, actions, and perspectives, as well as those of the tradition. It respects the integrity of both. Theological reflection therefore may confirm, challenge, clarify, and expand how we understand our own experience and how we understand the religious tradition. The outcome is new truth and meaning for living.[8]

While the above quotation was written from a Roman Catholic perspective, what it says about theological reflection can be extended with appropriate modifications to other religious traditions, because the structure of the art of theological reflection is, according to Killen, a dialogical process with five interdependent movements: (1) through reading a text one enters his or her *experience* and (2) encounters *feelings* or *emotional responses* engendered by the text; (3) paying attention to these feelings generates *images*; (4) attending to and questioning images may lead to *insight*; (5) insight leads, if we are willing, to *action*, part of the meaning of which for me is "social engagement."[9]

The art of theological reflection is not identical with academic theology, although my commitment to academic theological discourse continues to contextualize my particular practice of theological reflection. Nor is the art of theological reflection identical with what Catholic monastic theology calls *lectio divina* ("divine reading"), although there are similarities. Specifically, I tend to focus on Christian and non-Christian texts as well as remembered conversations and experiences that seem to me transformative. Part of my practice is to read the New Testament through once a year, usually in the summer when I have more quiet time, guided by a single question.[10] My reasons are both scholarly and personal: I think historians of religions must first understand and appreciate their own religious tradition before they are in a position to adequately understand and appreciate religious traditions other than their own. Furthermore, practice needs to be grounded in the foundational traditions of one's community.

I also include the Psalms and other texts from the Hebrew Bible as objects of theological reflection, as well as Buddhist texts like Śāntideva's *Bodhicaryāvatāra* ("Entering the Path of Enlightenment"), the writings of Martin Luther and Martin Luther King Jr., the poetry of William Butler Yeats and T. S. Eliot, the writings of Thich Nhat Hanh and Annie Dillard, the journals of Thomas Merton, and, most recently, the mystical theology of thirteenth-century women mystics like Marguerite Porete. The writings of John Cobb, Wilfred Cantwell Smith, Huston Smith, and John Hick; the novels of Mark Twain, John Steinbeck, and my friend Jack Cady; the Buddhist reflections of Sallie King and Rita Gross; the poetry of some of my students; the theology of religions of Paul Knitter—so deeply energized by his passion for social engagement—are also examples of texts I have appropriated for theological reflection.

For me, the process involves keeping a journal, since I am convinced that writing itself is a mode of meditation and that for those brought up in literate cultures, we never adequately understand a thing until we write it down. I do not engage in this practice expecting specific experiences or insights. Instead, I try to allow the process to take me where it takes me, like going on a journey without a destination or map. So as I read a text during this practice I begin by reflecting on the experience the text occasions and try to accurately describe its inner and outer dimensions—what the particular experience is to me and its objective content—in order to be fully aware of the source and nature of the experience. In other words, the intent is to attend to the experience's positive, negative, or neutral "emotional tone," in Japanese, its *mono no aware*,[11] by nonjudgmentally describing it, simply noting what the feelings are, in order to live consciously "inside" the experience, because this is the best position from which to reflect on the experience's meaning.

By entering an experience and narrating it nonjudgmentally, one discovers that it is drenched with feeling. This is so—probably in disagreement with standard Buddhist teaching—because our capacity to feel, to respond with our entire being to reality, is the essence of our nature as enfleshed persons. As such, feelings are embodied affective and intelligent responses to reality as we encounter it, so that feelings join mind and body and are the most human responses to reality. That is, through feelings, we encounter reality incarnated in our lives.[12]

This aspect of theological reflection, then, involves paying close attention to feelings because they embody a holistic response to our existence and are a source of creative insight. It is a process full of promise and, often, full of danger. The danger comes in two ways: (1) being overwhelmed and mired in feelings so that we subjectively grovel in them, or (2) being deadened to them. Both responses block insight. So the stage of attending to feelings involves being aware of them, without denying them or clinging to them, so that they can be identified clearly and accurately.

The next step involves giving shape and voice to feelings in the language of symbolic imagery. People do this in normal conversation all the time, as, for example, when my grandfather would say of a person he thought was ignorant, "He wouldn't know sheep shit from raisins if it was in the same pie," or when a sad person says "I feel like a motherless child," or when someone describes her friend as "having a heart of gold." Images work differently than conceptual descriptions. Images are more total, more closely tied to feelings, and less rationalized. Images create ways for feelings to be included in our world of meaning, thereby expanding our world by more immediate inclusion of new experience.

Sometimes musing on an image pushes us to new insights and frees us to respond to reality in ways never before imagined because images can compress many aspects of a situation into an integrated, intense wholeness, and, at the same time, open us to new angles of vision. In the process, images help us break free from habitual ways of interpreting our lives by propelling us to discover new meanings. At other times, pondering an image leads to unexpected surprises. That is, images can capture the core of a situation by shifting from the original descriptive narrative to a symbolic structure. In this way, they can engender insights and open doors to new ways of apprehension and self-awareness. Powerful insights can also engender action in the form of social engagement, consideration of which will be given after a brief description of centering prayer.[13]

Centering prayer is a method of refining one's intuitive faculties so that one is ready for the grace of contemplative prayer, which Thomas Keating describes as developing one's relationship with God to the point of communing beyond words, thoughts, feelings, and the multiplication of acts; "a process of moving from the simplified activity of waiting upon God to the ever-increasing predominance of the Gifts of the Spirit as the source of one's prayer."[14]

Centering prayer has much in common with certain aspects of Buddhist meditation, especially *zazen*, since unlike theological reflection, centering prayer is a discipline designed to withdraw attention from the ordinary flow of conscious thoughts and feelings through which we tend to identify our selves. It aims to expand awareness of a deeper dimension of selfhood, a dimension not completely sayable in words, yet one to which words can symbolically point. Mahayana Buddhists call this dimension of selfhood the "true Self." According to Christian mystical theology, the true Self is the image of God in which every human being—and, in my opinion, every thing—is created. So centering prayer, as I understand it, is a method of deepening the experience of interdependence, which, in Christian teaching, is affirmed theologically by the doctrines of creation and incarnation. Traditional Catholic theology understands centering prayer as preparatory to "contemplation," that process whereby the *image* of God incarnated in us as our true Self is transformed by grace into a *likeness* of God, so that we might apprehend the created universe as God apprehends it and love all things accordingly.

The technical details of my particular practice of centering prayer are fairly simple. For two thirty-minute periods a day—morning and evening—I take a comfortable sitting position in a quiet place while avoiding positions that cut off circulation so that bodily discomfort will not block concentration. I begin by taking a few deep breaths, and, while breathing slowly and evenly, I shut my eyes and begin withdrawing my senses from ordinary activity. With closed eyes, I bring to conscious attention what Thomas Keaton calls a "sacred word" that expresses my intention of opening and surrendering to God. I don't repeat this word aloud, but rather use it as an interior object of concentration.

The purpose here is not to suppress conscious thoughts and feelings, because that is not possible. The intention is to "observe" thoughts and feelings as they pass in review without stopping them or holding on to them. Whenever I catch myself holding on to a thought or feeling, I try to gently bring the sacred word into conscious focus until the thought or idea moves on. In this way, as the stream of conscious thoughts and feelings is quieted, one gradually becomes centered and open to whatever there is beyond the limitations of thoughts and our emotional responses to them.

For me, then, centering prayer is essentially an exercise in letting go, a method of allowing, without forcing, my ordinary train of thoughts and feelings to flow out. It is a kind of waiting without expectation designed to bring the interdependence of the present moment fully and consciously into focal awareness. According to Keating, practicing centering prayer with expectations or goals takes us out of the present and projects us into an imagined future that is most probably a reflection of our present ego trips. So centering prayer is a method of waking up to the presence of God in, with, and under the present interdependent moment without attachment to or anxiety about the future. Thomas Merton described this practice as "Entering the Silence"[15]—a process that does not require being a monk or a nun and, from both a Christian and Buddhist perspective, always energizes social engagement.

One of the important lessons I have learned from students and colleagues who are practiced in social engagement is that interreligious dialogue is not merely an abstract conversation between religious persons on this or that doctrine. Interreligious dialogue—as well as the practice of theological reflection and centering prayer—requires involvement in the hard realities of historical, political, and economic existence. Or, to paraphrase the Epistle of James, "theological reflection, centering prayer, and interreligious dialogue without works are dead" for the same reasons that "faith without works is dead." For me, a central point of the practice of faith is the liberation of human beings and all creatures in nature from forces of oppression and injustice and the mutual creative transformation of persons in community with nature. Both the wisdom that Buddhists affirm is engendered by Awakening and the Christian doctrines of creation and incarnation point to the utter interdependency of all things and events at every moment of space-time—a notion also affirmed by contemporary physics and biology in distinctively scientific terms.[16] Awareness of interdependency, in turn, engenders social engagement, because interdependence and social engagement are themselves interdependent. Thus we experience the suffering of others as our suffering, the oppression of others as our oppression, the oppression of nature as our oppression, and the liberation of others as our liberation—and thereby we become empowered for social engagement.

Consequently, any religious practice needs to include focus on practical issues that are not religion-specific or culture-specific, that is, issues that confront all human beings regardless of what religious or secular label they wear. In this regard, my running thesis about practice is in agreement with Christians like Martin Luther, Martin Luther King Jr., and Mother Theresa; the Vietnamese Buddhist monk Thich Nhat Hanh and the Thai Buddhist layman Sulak Siveraksa; the Hindu sage and activist Mahatma Gandhi; as well as Jewish and Islamic calls that we struggle for justice in obedience to Torah or surrender to Allah guided by the *Qur'an*. They all insist that religious faith and practice do not separate us from the world. The practice of faith throws us *into* the world's struggle for peace and justice; any practice that refuses to wrestle with the world's injustices is as impotent as it is self-serving. Accordingly, whatever practice we follow needs to be guided by a concern for the liberation of all sentient beings, for, as both Christian and Buddhist teachings affirm, we are all in this together. Distinctively Christian practices, and, I suspect, distinctively Buddhist practices of social engagement—the topic of the next chapter—cannot have it any other way, because in an interdependently processive universe, there is no other way.

ENDNOTES

[1] See my book, *Wrestling With the Ox: A Theology of Religious Experience* (New York: Continuum, 1997).

[2] This is a modified restatement of an observation by George Santanya. See *Interpretations of Poetry and Religion* (New York: Harper Torchbooks, 1957) chapter 9.

[3] See Robert Traer, "Faith in the Buddhist Tradition," *Buddhist-Christian Studies* 11 (1991) 85–120.

[4] See Paul O. Ingram and Frederick J. Streng, editors, *Buddhist-Christian Dialogue: Essays in Mutual Renewal and Transformation* (Honolulu: University of Hawaii Press, 1986) 53–74.

[5] Ibid., 54–55.

[6] I have made note of these parallels in several past publications. See my *The Dharma of Faith* (Washington, D.C.: University Press of America, 1977) chapter 4; "Shinran Shonin and Martin Luther: A Soteriological Comparison," *Journal of the American Academy of Religion* 39 (1971) 447–80.

[7] Ingram and Strange, *Buddhist-Christian Dialogue*, 54.

[8] Patricia O'Connell Killen and John de Beer, *The Art of Theological Reflection* (New York: Crossroad, 1994) viii.

[9] Ibid., chapter 2.

[10] My fellow historian of religions and fellow participant in Buddhist-Christian dialogue, Terry Muck, introduced me to this practice over dinner in New Orleans in 1999. My question for that year was engendered by the death of my father in April: What does the Jesus saying, "To live your life you must first lose it," mean?

[11] *Mono no aware,* or "the feeling of things," is a fundamental principle of Japanese aesthetics that has also played a crucial role in Japanese religious history. Thus what an artist portrays—in painting, poetry, or literature—is not a literal photographic-like representation of an object or experience but its "feeling-tone" as experienced by the artist and communicated to viewers or readers, without passing moral judgments on the feelings portrayed. So when viewing a painting or reading or hearing a poem, we

are brought into the experience of the artist as he or she creates. It is the *mono no aware* of an object or experience that reveals its reality, that is, its "suchness," to appropriate a Zen Buddhist phrase.

[12] Killen and de Beer, *The Art of Theological Reflection,* chapter 2.

[13] Ibid.

[14] Thomas Keating, *Open Mind, Open Heart: The Contemplative Dimension of the Gospel* (New York: Continuum, 1997) 146.

[15] Thomas Merton, *Entering the Silence: Becoming a Monk & a Writer,* The Journals of Thomas Merton 2, ed. Jonathan Montaldo (San Francisco: Harper, 1996).

[16] See Arthur Peacocke, *Theology for a Scientific Age: Being and Becoming—Natural, Divine and Human* (Minneapolis: Fortress, 1993) 39–43 for a wonderful summary of the current consensus among scientists regarding the interdependent and interconnected structure of the physical universe.

Chapter 4

Socially Engaged Buddhist-Christian Dialogue

I am often annoyed by uncritical caricatures some Christian scholars regularly foist upon Buddhist tradition. In more charitable moments, I think such caricatures are unintentional, their purposes usually benign. Most Christians engaged in serious dialogue with Buddhists have no explicit evangelical agenda. Yet caricatures persist in scholarly Christian discourse about Buddhist tradition. Since these caricatures often occur in the work of Christians who admire Buddhist tradition and seek to learn from it, they are all the more disturbing—at least to me.

One caricature that still haunts Christian encounter with Buddhist faith and practice is the assumption that Buddhist tradition as a whole is socially unengaged, and therefore in need of serious reformation through dialogue with Christian tradition. Important Buddhist teachers and philosophers have also bought into this caricature. For example, Masao Abe, in relation to justice issues, writes:

> But some Buddhist thinkers, including myself, are aware that Buddhism must develop itself through confrontation with Christianity. It may not be related to the most fundamental point. But with such problems as that of justice and the understanding of history in regard to justice, I

think Buddhists must learn from Christianity, because the idea of justice is very weak and unclear in Buddhism.[1]

Christopher S. Queen agrees. He describes "socially engaged Buddhism" as a new "fourth *yana*" or "vehicle," alongside the three older main traditions of Buddhism called Theravada ("School of the Elders," mostly identified with the Buddhism of South Asia), Mahayana ("Great Vehicle," mostly identified with the Buddhism of East Asia), and Vajrayana ("Diamond Vehicle," identified with Tibetan and Central Asian Buddhism).[2] Queen believes that socially engaged Buddhism is "new Buddhism" because:

The direction of contemporary Buddhism, like other ancient faith traditions, has been deeply influenced by both the magnitude of social suffering in the world today and by the globalization of cultural values and perspectives we associate with Western cultural tradition, especially, the notions of human rights, economic justice, political due process, and social progress.[3]

In other words, socially engaged Buddhism is a new form of Buddhism that has since the 1960s been emerging out of Western democratic thought and social justice traditions. It embodies currents of teaching and practice that, while not absent from classical Buddhist tradition, are radically new in Buddhism's growing influence in Western societies. In Queen's view, nothing comparable to this "new Buddhism" ever happened in non-Western Buddhist traditions.[4]

A more nuanced interpretation of this view of Buddhist tradition is also at work in the theology of Abe's main Christian dialogical partner, John Cobb. In comparing the ethical and social implications of Buddhist and Christian "universalism," Cobb notes that despite many striking parallels, Buddhist and Christian teachings make different universal claims. According to Buddhist teaching, Gautama is one of many embodiments of the Buddha Nature, so that the once-and-for-all uniqueness of the historical Jesus is not asserted about the historical Buddha.[5] The claim that the Buddha Nature is in all things and events—a Mahayana, not a Theravada teaching, be it noted—and that the Awakening attained by Gautama is the proper goal of all sentient beings is not the same as

Christian claims about the resurrection. That is, the "structure of Buddhist existence" is not the same as the "structure of Christian existence."[6]

This implies, for Cobb, that Buddhist practice and experience have broken the "dominance of the self" or the "I" because all boundaries and distinctions between self and other are ontologically canceled at the moment of Awakening. In so doing, Buddhist experience frees persons from anxiety and egoistic self-concern. Thereby, Buddhists are able to achieve a unique openness to the structures of reality. Christian tradition, however, heightens self-transcendence by objectifying one's self as separate from other selves. Thus Christians are taught that individual selves can and should assume responsibility for what they do and for what they are. Consequently, Cobb thinks there is fuller ethical and social consciousness in the structure of Christian experience than in the structure of Buddhist experience.[7]

For this reason, in Cobb's opinion, the Christian notion of *agape* is different from the Buddhist notion of *karuṇā*. In Mahayana tradition especially, when non-attachment is attained, the Bodhisattva is thereby filled with compassionate empathy for the suffering of all unenlightened sentient beings. But even though this is a "beautiful idea," Cobb thinks the Christian notion of *agape* is ethically more sensitive to issues of social justice. *Agape*, he writes, centers on awareness of selves involved with, yet ontologically independent of, other selves. It also implies ontological separation between human selves and the self of God. Since selves in separation from God are in a state of sin, no self can become virtuous through living an ethically good life. However a morally good life might be conceived, sinful selves do not establish it in relation to other selves or to God by any form of moral behavior or social activism. Since salvation is a gift of God's graceful *agape*, moral and social behavior is "Christian" only if it expresses gratitude for what God's loving grace has bestowed on the self. That is, while Christians have moral and social obligations to be performed as expressions of gratitude, performing moral and social obligations do not make one "good," since all selves, even selves graced by God, remain in a state of sin.

Consequently, *agape* seems to Cobb to be less "defused" than *karuṇā*, and therefore ethically and socially more relevant to the life experiences of selves existing separately, yet interactively, in the world. It is, therefore, his judgment that *agape* has historically provided norms of ethical and social organization that are more fully developed in Christian traditions of social justice than in Buddhist tradition.[8]

It must be emphasized that Cobb's point is not that actual Buddhists are less moral or less loving than actual Christians. His point is that as Christian faith can be theologically transformed by appropriating Buddhist denials of substance categories in reference to the self, so Buddhist tradition can be ethically transformed by appropriating Christian notions of transcendence and can thereby deepen its tradition of social activism, the Buddhist word for which is "social engagement."[9]

While at first glance there seems to be much in the formative Theravada and Mahayana lineages of Buddhism that supports these views, I shall argue that Buddhist traditions of social engagement, while conceived differently from Christian ethical-social teaching, has historically been at the heart of Buddhist teaching, practice, and experience. That is, ethics and social engagement have played as important a role in Buddhist teaching and practice as ethics and social activism have played in Christian teaching and practice. Indeed, Buddhist "awakening" is never an unethical event that withdraws an awakened one from engagement with the needs of society at large. The same is true for the practice of Christian faith: salvation is never an unethical or socially unengaged event.

Since what contemporary Buddhists mean by "social engagement" is interconnected with distinctively Buddhist traditions of ethics, it seems prudent to analyze three "obstacles" in Western philosophical ethical reflection that George Dreyfus thinks hinder Western appreciation of the role of ethics in Buddhist thought and experience.[10] I shall argue that these same obstacles also distort much Christian—and Buddhist—understanding and appreciation of the role played by social engagement in Buddhist tradition as a whole. This will be followed by a summary description of traditions of engaged Buddhist practice in Theravada and Mahayana lineages prior to Thich Nhat Hanh's first use of "socially engaged Buddhism" to describe his non-violent anti-war movement in Vietnam. But first, let me make some preliminary observations.

"Engaged Buddhism" is a relatively recent term that describes Buddhist social activism. It was first used by Thich Naht Hanh in 1963 in a book he wrote entitled *Engaged Buddhism.*[11] As defined in another book Thich Naht Hanh wrote during the Vietnam War entitled *Lotus in a Sea of Fire,* the focus of "engaged Buddhism" is the creation of a nonaligned, nonbelligerent Buddhist anti-war coalition, which he described as "an enemy of neither combatant."[12] In subsequent works he wrote that Buddhist tradition has always been "socially engaged, so that his anti-war movement was not new in Buddhist history."[13]

Because of the growing popularity of Thich Naht Hanh's thought, both Buddhists and Christians, especially in Europe and the United States, picked up this term as a designation and description of something that had not occurred before in Buddhist history. So the first question to be addressed is why this should be the case. Is there anything new in "engaged Buddhism" that has not been characteristic of previous Buddhist history? I shall argue that while the term "engaged Buddhism" is new, it points to traditions of ethical discipline and social activism that have always been central to Buddhist thought and practice. What *is* new about "engaged Buddhism" is what this term means in its present contemporary context.[14] To see this, it is necessary to engage in a critique of traditional Western assumptions about ethics that predominate in Western philosophy and currently govern most Christian ethical and social thought.

Three Western Obstacles

As George Dreyfus notes, even when Western interpreters notice that Buddhist meditational practices are relevant to ethical self-discipline and social engagement, they incorrectly tend to view social activism as something quite external to Buddhist experience of awakening. Thus, most Christians interpret *śīla* ("morality") mainly as a set of injunctions to avoid certain kinds of conduct, such as the five precepts emphasized in Theravada tradition or the ten virtues emphasized in Tibetan tradition. These injunctions help Buddhists gradually withdraw from the world into a private experience of an Awakening that detaches individuals from social and worldly care. Three assumptions seem to guide this view.

First, most contemporary Western ethical theories assert that ethics is primarily about rules and injunctions, while less concerned with the development of good character. This assumption is particularly common to utilitarian theories, which emphasize choosing the right course of action for the sake of the greatest happiness for the greatest number. Notions of injunctions and rightness are also emphasized in deontological theories.

Deontology, associated with Kant, holds that the goodness of moral life does not consist in the development of human qualities such as good character, but consists in the ability to act according to universal moral laws. Thus, to be moral is to decide to act upon certain agreed upon rules of action—the maxims that conform to these universal moral laws.

Second, most contemporary ethical theory asserts the duality of reason and emotion, along with the privileging of reason. This dualism is also strongly characteristic in Kantian traditions of ethical theory. We cannot help what we feel, but only what we do. So no one can be said to have a duty to feel certain emotions or to act from certain emotions. Ethics must be understood as a system of obligations. Since emotions cannot be made objects of obligations, they are without ethical relevance. Neither their presence nor their absence can reflect on a person's morality, since they are outside the scope of personal responsibility. Seen from this point of view, ethics becomes the exploration of the rationality of limited decisions reached through weighing the advantages or disadvantages of alternatives, all in isolation from human emotional experiences and human participation in religious or cultural traditions.

Third, most contemporary Western ethical theory asserts a duality between external agency and internal attitudes. Here again, the Kantian tradition is representative of the widely shared Western view that ethics concerns the domain of external action, not the realm of internal emotions. So ethics and social activism become a matter of thinking clearly and then proceeding to outward dealings with other human beings. But the attitudes we have or the emotions we experience in these dealings are ethically irrelevant. To be moral does not mean to possess good human qualities, as in most traditional cultures and in Buddhist tradition, but to choose the right course of action.

Accordingly, since the aim of Buddhist ethics is to *become* virtuous, not merely to adhere to objective moral rules arrived at rationally, Western virtue ethics approaches—those that originate in Platonic and Aristotelian philosophy rather than utilitarian or deontological approaches—might provide Christians a more useful hermeneutical bridge from which to conduct a dialogue with Buddhist traditions of social engagement. Accordingly, as a "thought experiment," I shall employ a virtue ethics approach as a heuristic device through which to examine and interpret the ethical sources of traditional Buddhist activism, now referred to as Buddhist social engagement.

The Broad Historical Context: Theravada and Mahayana Traditions

The earliest Pali traditions of Buddhist ethics clearly pay attention to achieving virtue.[15] Ethics is about the "good life," meaning a life oriented towards a good end through social engagement. That is, in common with, but not identical to, Greek traditions of virtue ethics, the *telos* ("orientation") of Buddhist ethics and social engagement is *eudaimonia*, or happiness and well-being, in which "the good" is a whole made up of interlocking and interrelated parts in accordance with the practice of certain virtues.[16] This is so because Buddhist moral life and social engagement, like everything else in Buddhist tradition, is grounded in the teaching of *pratītya-samutpāda*, or "dependent co-origination."[17]

This is clearly the emphasis of the Pali Canon. Yet on the surface, the majority of passages in the Pali texts seem to present the meaning of Buddhist practice as escape from the world and its social involvements. Certainly, these texts say very little about the world's renewal or changing society's social structures. World renewal and social change seem left to the impersonally operating cyclic forces of *saṃsāra* flowing according to the Law of Karma. Thus, the truly Buddhist method of interrelating with the world and society is to form an order of monks—a society within a larger society, yet apart from this larger society—in hope of attaining awakened freedom (*nibbāna*) from all worldly attachments.[18]

But this picture, while a large part of the Pali texts, is not the whole picture. Theravada literature presents a much broader conception of Buddhist goals and practices that are not often acknowledged either by contemporary Mahayana Buddhists or Christians engaged in dialogue with Buddhists. In fact, the Pali Canon describes three goals of Buddhist practice, all of which are said to be "good."[19] On the lowest level is the practice of ethical precepts such as the five precepts in order to achieve a more positive future rebirth. This is the traditional goal of Theravada Buddhist laypersons, and is considered by the Pali texts to be limited and provisional, its purpose being to move the mind away from attachment to worldly concerns and in the process achieve better rebirths in future lives.

On the highest level is the goal of arhathood, the state of a person liberated from the causes of suffering through the practice of "morality" (*śīla*), "wisdom" (*pranna*), and "insight" (*jhāna*). One achieving this state has attained the perfection of knowledge and compassion. It is the attainment of a certain level of moral excellence. Buddhists who reach this level embrace, in the process, certain social goals. Furthermore, these goals all share common fundamental virtues that constitute the "good life": a life of compassionate, yet detached, social activism in which human beings, first and foremost, are concerned with the well-being and flourishing of all sentient beings and who express this compassionate concern within the realities of social, political, and economic existence, which constitutes the intermediate level.[20]

Consequently, monks and laity are ethically and socially interdependent in their Buddhist practice; each needs the other and must serve the other in the creation of an ideal community called the *saṃgha*. Monks need food and shelter and depend on the laity for their efforts to achieve *nibbānic*, that is, "enlightened" or "awakened," freedom from society. But monks are expected to teach the *dhamma* to lay persons, work to relieve their suffering, and to model the virtues of Buddhist practice, even though laypersons must remain in the secular world. Thus the practice of virtues for monks—the third intermediate level—entails wise and compassionate engagement with the world, while remaining detached from the world, which I interpret to mean "being in the world, but not of the world." That is, Theravada traditions of social engagement provide guidance for virtuous social conduct through the cultivation of nonviolence.

However, the traditions of Buddhist social engagement did not end with the Theravada tradition. During the two thousand or more years that the Buddhist Way spread to China, Tibet, Korea, and Japan, an extensive body of Mahayana ethical and social teachings evolved that produced ideals that continue to undergird Buddhist social engagement today. The key to this expansion is specifically Mahayana interpretations of the doctrine of "dependent co-origination" (*pratītya-samutpāda*) as this teaching interrelates with the Bodhisattva concept along with the resulting importance given to the significance of Buddhist laypersons.

To state the matter perhaps too simply, the Bodhisattva, "one whose being is Awakening," a "Buddha-in-the-making," became every person's ideal in Mahayana teaching about achieving the good life-in-community. Here, the usual Theravada ideal of the secluded monk, "wandering alone in the forest like a rhinoceros" until he achieves awakened detachment that allows him to be engaged with the world while not being of the world, was replaced by a different ideal: the Buddhist monk, nun, or layperson who through endless deeds of wisdom and compassion though numerous cycles of rebirth strove for Buddhahood by vowing to help all sentient beings attain Awakening.

My favorite Mahayana text that describes the good life as compassionate wisdom in social engagement with all sentient beings-in-community is Śāntideva's *Bodhicaryāvatāra* [Entering the Path of Awakening]:

> May I too, through whatever good I have accomplished by doing all this, become one who works for the complete alleviation of the sufferings of all beings.

> May I be medicine for the sick; may I also be their physician and attend them until their disease no longer recurs. With showers of food and water, may I eliminate the pain of hunger and thirst, and during the intermediate periods of great famine between eons, may I be food and drink.

> And may I be an inexhaustible storehouse for the poor, and may I always be first in being ready to serve them in various ways.

> So that all beings may achieve their aims, may I sacrifice, without regret, the bodies as well as the pleasures I have had and the merit of all the good that I have accomplished and will accomplish in the past, present, and future.

> Nirvana means to renounce everything. My mind is set on nirvana, so because I am to renounce everything, it is best to give it to others.[21]

Another example of the Mahayana ideal of social engagement grounded in the teaching of dependent co-origination is portrayed in the

Vimalakīrti Sūtra (The Discourse of the Layman Vimalakīrti). In this text, one of the most popular in Mahayana literature, Vimalakīrti is described by Gautama the Buddha as a sort of "super-bodhisattva" who even surpasses the Buddha's own disciples in wisdom and virtue. He is fully awakened as a lay Bodhisattva thoroughly involved in the rough-and-tumble of society, whose compassionate wisdom exceeds that of cloistered monks and nuns. As the sutra describes him:

> At that time there lived in the city of Vaisali a certain Licchavi, Vimalakīrti by name. . . . He wore the white clothes of a layman, yet lived impeccably like a religious devotee. He lived at home, but remained aloof from the realm of desire. . . . He had a son, a wife, and female attendants, yet always maintained continence. . . . He seemed to eat and drink, yet always took nourishment from meditation. He made his appearance in the fields of sports and casinos, yet his aim was always to mature those people who were attached to games and gambling.[22]

In business, in government affairs, equally at home with teachers, warriors, politicians, and ordinary folk, all without spiritual and moral ethical compromise, Vimalakīrti models the highest ideal, for laypersons and ordained monks and nuns, of Buddhist ethical virtue (*śīla*) expressed through compassionate social engagement with all sentient beings. Understanding this assertion requires a brief description of how Mahayana tradition expanded the meaning of *śīla* in terms of its distinctive interpretation of dependent co-origination and the Bodhisattva ideal.

As in Theravada thought, roughly speaking, there are three levels of *śīla* in Mahayana teaching and practice. In many ways, these levels are similar to Theravada understanding, but their meanings are stretched beyond their Theravada origins. The first level of Mahayana *śīla* focuses on moral injunctions, the keeping of moral precepts and rules to ward off immoral faults and actions. These "faults," as discussed in detail in the Vinaya literature, fall into two categories: (1) "natural faults" and (2) "conventional faults." "Natural faults" are actions, such as killing or lying, that are karmically negative and directly harm others and the person who does them, regardless of who they are. Anyone engaging in such acts is not virtuous and generates negative karma.

"Conventional faults" are incurred by disobeying conventional moral injunctions. For example, for lay Buddhists, eating a meal after noon is not an ethical issue. For monks and nuns, however, eating after noon constitutes a moral fault because of the conventional rules that apply to their lives when they accept ordination. Among these two types of faults, natural faults are more important. Thus for all Buddhists, "morality" is defined as the resolution to abstain from harming others.

The second meaning of *śīla* in Mahayana tradition is more ethically inclusive. Here, *śīla* entails the whole range of virtuous practices in which a person engages after making a commitment to achieve Awakening for the sake of all sentient beings. Anyone making this commitment is a Bodhisattva; for such persons, Bodhisattva practices like patience, giving, contemplation, and meditation are forms of *śīla*. But this form of practice is beyond moral injunctions. That is, for the Bodhisattva, *śīla* is not keeping the precepts in a legalistic way. The practice of *śīla* is living the good life in accordance with the practices of virtues. Thus it is not enough for a Bodhisattva to merely refrain from specific acts of violence; the Bodhisattva must become nonviolent through the practice of non-violence.

Finally, the third level of Mahayana conceptions of *śīla* goes beyond the domain of moral injunctions and relates directly to the life of the Bodhisattva as modeled by Vimalakīrti. At this level, *śīla* is identical with "social engagement." The Bodhisattva, working for the sake of all sentient beings, is compassionately focused on service to others: nursing the sick, leading the blind, helping the oppressed, providing food and clothing for the poor. This level of Mahayana *śīla* is interesting for two reasons: (1) it dispels the misconception that Buddhist faith and practice promotes self-involvement, and (2) it clearly demonstrates the importance of socially engaged service to all beings in Buddhist tradition.

The third level of Mahayana *śīla* practice is also more evident in Mahayana tradition than the second level. Though intended for Bodhisattvas, the ethics of collecting virtues can be extended to other Buddhist practices. This is not so with the ethics of helping others. Although similar practices are indeed recommended in Theravada tradition, these are subordinate to attaining Awakening for oneself. Here, Mahayana tradition differs: helping others is a goal of practice in and of itself, since in an interdependent universe, no one is fully awakened until all are fully awakened. Likewise, as the suffering of one person diminishes all persons, so the Awakening of any Buddha engenders wise compassionate benefit for all suffering sentient beings. No one is fully liberated from suffering unless all beings are liberated; no one is fully awakened unless all beings are awakened. We are all interdependently together in this universe.

Consequently, at this third level, Mahayana tradition emphasizes that the Bodhisattva's compassion is aimed at helping others—not merely to develop concern for others, but to actively help others. The Bodhisattva's "wisdom"—knowledge that reality is so interdependent that there is no separation from self and others—engenders compassionate social engagement that aims to relieve all sentient beings from suffering within the institutional structures of social, political, and economic existence.

Concrete examples of the practice of compassionate social engagement mark the political histories of both Theravada and Mahayana traditions. For example, Asoka Maurya's conversion to Buddhism in the third century BC began the spread of Buddhism as a state religion across South Asia and the creation of Buddhist centered civilizations. This "Asokan ideal"[23] became a justification for political activism everywhere in Asia and continues today in South Asia where criticism of government leaders in Sri Lanka, Thailand, and Burma is still "significantly most effective" when "they are charged with being un-Buddhist." Donald Swearer notes how in contemporary times the Venerable Buddhadasa continued the Asokan ideal in the model community he established in northern Thailand where his students still carry on his "harmonious, non-competitive" Buddha-dharma that emphasizes interdependence, restraint, and generosity.[24] The political activism of Buddhadasa's lay disciple, Sulak Sivaraksa, against the Thai government's exploitation of its people represents a continuation of the Asokan ideal of non-violent struggle for social, political, and economic justice.

The Asokan ideal is also exemplified by the history of Mahayana tradition. In China, Korea, and Japan, Buddhist social and political engagement brought the Dharma out of the monastery and into society and statecraft. One need only study the histories of Chinese Buddhist social engagement during the T'ang and Sung Dynasties,[25] the social roles of Buddhist institutions in Korea to relieve the suffering of the poor and those oppressed by authoritarian governmental policies,[26] or the political and social activism on behalf of the politically and economically exploited by the "Kamakura" schools of "reform" Buddhism—Zen, Jodo Shu, Jodo

58

Shinshu, and Nichiren Shu—in Japan from the thirteenth to the fifteenth centuries to see the Asokan ideal at work in Buddhist history.[27]

In the late sixties, it was Buddhist political activism, led by the Vietnamese Zen monk Tri Quang, that brought down the oppressive government of Ngo Dinh Diem in spite of American support,[28] a tradition of non-violent social engagement continued by Thich Naht Hanh. So too is the Asokan ideal at work in the contemporary Won Buddhist movement, founded by the Korean monk Sot'aesan (1891–1943), whose members and leaders continue the founder's struggle for world peace through not only interreligious dialogue, but through social engagement with the political, social, and economic forces that engender world wide violence.[29] Finally, no Buddhist movement in America deserves more praise for its social activism and struggle against racial oppression and its non-violent work for world peace than Soka Gakkai International.[30]

In an interdependent universe, then, what is the defining principle of Buddhist social engagement? It can only be the first of the Five Precepts: "non-violence."[31] The most persuasive recent Western discussion of contemporary Buddhist socially engaged non-violence is a collection of eight essays edited by Kenneth Kraft entitled *Inner Peace, World Peace: Essays on Buddhism and Nonviolence*.[32] Kraft's essay in this volume notes that because individual greed, hatred, and delusion are the central human problems from which all need deliverance, he affirms Thich Nhat Hanh's statement, "social work entails inner work."[33] That is, social reform pursued merely from a socio-ideological or an economic-ideological point of view will at best provide only temporary solutions to social and economic issues, and at worst perpetuate the very ills social reform aims to cure. This is the fundamental principle of every form of distinctively Buddhist social engagement. The inner motivations of reformers must always be kept under close scrutiny—by reformers and by those they seek to reform. Or stated more positively, distinctively Buddhist social engagement assumes a "virtue ethics" orientation that is engendered by the practice of meditation. In the processes of meditative and ethical self-discipline, one *becomes* virtuous and exercises virtue in social engagement with political and economic realities in the hard struggle for community.

There is, of course, great diversity of Buddhist opinion about the meaning and application of this principle. Thich Naht Hanh is sometimes understood to have a quietist view of Buddhist social engagement.

One's mind must become non-violent in social engagement for world peace. Consequently, he stresses that meditative practice is as necessary for Buddhist social engagement as social engagement is for meditative practice.[34]

Robert Thurman thinks the Dalai Lama's philosophy of non-violence is the operating principle of Tibetan Buddhist notions of the ideal social order. The Dalai Lama prays for the Chinese who invaded and still occupy Tibet because even violent oppressors must be objects of compassion. He never ceases to point out that because the world is filled with violence, it is perfectly arranged to promote humanity's compassionate development. Indeed, he constantly teaches that in an interdependent world of suffering beings, toward whom is there not ample opportunity to exercise compassionate social engagement?[35]

Finally, Sulak Sivaraksa is, by Western standards, the most activist of the examples of Buddhist social engagement I have noted, mostly because of his social and political activities in Thailand—at considerable personal risk—and because his views are explicitly political in nature. He writes: "The Buddhist approach to peace demands self-awareness and social awareness in equal measure."[36] Accordingly, while meditation loosens the hold of personal and social prejudice, the Five Precepts—not to kill, not to steal, to speak the truth, to abstain from illicit sexuality, to avoid intoxicants—must be interpreted in realistic and flexible terms. For example, Sulak interprets non-killing to include seeking remedies in situations in which some persons live in rich abundance while others live in poverty. Speaking the truth refers equally to personal truthfulness and refraining from clinging (*taṇhā*) to ideologies in the mistaken notion that they are identical with unchanging truths. Avoiding intoxicants means engaging the social and economic conditions that make the Thai drug trade and sex industries profitable. He also believes that some sort of world government is congenial with Buddhist principles.

Some Concluding Observations

Often, as I have participated in dialogical discussions between Buddhists and Christians on such topics as the environment, justice, poverty, or violence, it is easier for me to identify a distinctively Buddhist position than a distinctively Christian position. Of course, the problem may be strictly my own. But I often have difficulty identifying what makes a particular form of social activism Christian and not something else, say, Jewish or Islamic" or Hindu. Buddhists seem as compassionate and as loving as Christians; Buddhists seem as concerned about justice, economic exploitation, and environmental degradation as Christians; Buddhists seem as concerned with world peace as Christians. Agapic love of one's neighbors can be, and often is, affirmed by Buddhists; compassion for all suffering beings is recognized and celebrated by many Christians.

I suspect my difficulty originates in the way in which Christian ethicists talk about social issues. Much of this talk seems to view Buddhist ethical theory and social engagement through the filter of Western utilitarian or deontological thought, rather than through Western virtue approaches. Furthermore, "Christian ethics" often seems to me more a matter of duty than of virtue, since the stress of much contemporary Christian discourse and social activism is on performing obligations consistent with the gift of God's love to humanity created by the events surrounding the historical Jesus.[37] Thus, from a Protestant perspective, at least, Christian ethics and social activism do not normally demand that persons become virtuous. Nor is meditation or contemplative prayer a required ingredient of ethical behavior or social activism. One does not often hear in Christian teaching that "outer work involves inner work."

The traditional Christian upshot seems something like this: sinful human beings in a sinful world can never become virtuous. But illumined by God's grace, sinful persons can recognize this existential context for making ethical and social choices and behave morally in social activism as an act of gratitude for what God has accomplished for humanity through the life, death, and resurrection of the historical Jesus. *But one need not be a Christian or experience Christian faith to live according to the moral obligations guiding Christian social activism.* There seems to be little that distinguishes Christian ethics and social activism from non-Christian ethics and social activism, so that what makes a moral choice or participation in social activism particularly Christian and not something else often escapes me.

I usually do not experience the same difficulty understanding what makes traditions of ethics and social engagement "Buddhist." Buddhist traditions of social engagement are bound to a specific worldview in which the doctrines of "dependent co-origination" and "non-self" are defining teachings that distinguish Buddhism from other religious traditions. Christian traditions of ethics and social activism are not as worldview specific. That is, the core of Buddhist ethics and social engagement is a strong sense of the intimate, organic interrelatedness of all sentient beings—a worldview upon which everything "Buddhist" depends. Accordingly, Buddhists are led from rigid absolutist distinctions that cut individuals off from creative social relationships in community to an openness that is fully aware of the dynamic interrelatedness of all things and events at every moment of space-time. Furthermore, awareness of interdependency does not blur awareness of differences of personal, social, and historical distinctions and identities. Rather, the experience of universal interdependence enables compassion to flow more freely in creative interaction with others through recognizing that while others are different, they remain tightly bound together in the universal web of interrelationships that constitute the whole of reality.

Perhaps a solution to my difficulties in understanding what makes Christian social engagement "Christian" and Buddhist social engagement "Buddhist" springs from a lesson I have learned from the history of religions: people understand reality through narratives. Religious traditions work through narratives and religious people constantly reinterpret these narratives, thereby gaining new insight to engage issues that a religious tradition's narratives could not have foreseen in their earlier histories. Sometimes these reinterpretations are performed by ignoring, or even rejecting, part of a tradition's narrative that is deemed irrelevant. Either way, understanding a religious tradition, one's own or someone else's, means grappling with its foundational narratives.[38]

It is their narratives that distinguish Christian and Buddhist traditions of social engagement. It is clear, at least to me, that contemporary Buddhist social activists have reclaimed aspects of the Dharma that have always existed in Buddhist tradition in order to address issues of injustice in a new way, just as Christian activists in the late nineteenth and early twentieth centuries focused on neglected aspects of the Bible to preach a social gospel of engagement with the world—a tradition continuing in Christian liberation and feminist theologies, minus the Social Gospel's optimism about human nature.

Of course, there are many more stories in Buddhism's narrative tradition than Christianity's narrative tradition. The number of texts comprising the Buddhist cannon is immense, more like a library. Christians have a one-volume narrative anthology—the Bible—and most of the narratives come from Hebrew texts. John Dominic Crossan has pointed out that Christian tradition transmuted its parables into moral allegories, while the original teller of the parables, Jesus, became the parable of God.[39] In other words, there is a basic Christian narrative about the world that is fundamentally eschatological in character. Christians experience the universe as moving toward a last age, to a final fulfillment, to what Teilhard de Chardin called the "Omega point." The universe is going somewhere, lured by God to achieve its final consummation. The value of the universe is for Christians grounded on the doctrine of Incarnation: in the life, death, and resurrection of Jesus of Nazareth, God took upon God's self the conditions of finite existence imposed by realities of history and biology, and continues doing so through the Holy Spirit until God's intention in creation is fulfilled. Of course there is a great deal of disagreement and discussion about this aspect of the Christian narrative within the history of Christian thought.

Buddhism's defining narratives present a very different vision of the universe, which I describe in chapter five in regard to Buddhist dialogue with the natural sciences. Buddhist thought does not place emphasis on the historical movement of the universe toward a final consummation. Indeed, Buddhist tradition celebrates the absence of teleological assumptions in its teachings. The doctrine of dependent co-origination, for example, teaches that existence commences with ignorance which leads to old age and death only to commence again through another rebirth in the constant turning of the wheel of samsaric suffering—until one achieves Awakening and the karma that binds one to the wheel of birth and death is finally overcome. Ideas such as these, it seems to me, leave little room for narrative history, the implication of which, for Buddhists, is that the universe in and of itself is purposeless and, like everything caught in the field of space-time, will eventually disappear. But the Christian narrative begins with a creation story and concludes with a final fulfillment, toward which all things and events in the universe are even now being lured.

Perhaps social engagement that is specifically "Christian" is to build a world of peace and justice for human beings and the creatures of nature within history, which for Christian faith and practice is the locus, the place where God's continual creative action in the world is taking place. Christians wrestle with God within historical events. In this sense, history is the Christian counterpart of what Buddhists mean by dependent co-arising, because historical processes are interdependent processes in which all things and events are interrelated.

Accordingly, the differences between Buddhist and Christian traditions of social engagement have more to do, I think, with the narrative assumptions underlying both traditions rather than differences between explicit doctrinal positions. The actual practice of Buddhist social engagement based on non-self, interdependence, and compassionate wisdom are not contrary to Christian experience or Christian social activist traditions based on faith active in love in the struggle for justice for all persons and for nature. Socially engaged Christian practice can easily harmonize Buddhists teachings of interdependence and compassion with the Christian demand to love all with no strings attached, which I have described as an ethic of loving/compassionate wisdom.

My concluding observations in this chapter are these: (1) Buddhist traditions of ethics and social activism are not less fully evolved than these traditions are in Christian experience; but they do assume different narratives. Nor are Buddhist traditions of ethics and social engagement more fully evolved than they are in Christian faith and experience; they merely rest upon different narrative visions of the structure of existence. (2) The question of which tradition is more ethically and socially engaged is neither important nor interesting. Therefore, it should not be a focus of Buddhist-Christian dialogue. (3) Buddhists and Christians share the same world and the same problems all religious human beings share: the necessity of being socially engaged with the systemic forces that endanger the human community along with all life on this planet. Consumerism, poverty, political oppression, racism, and ecological degradation of the environment are so serious in their present scope that differences in religious doctrines, while philosophically interesting, pale to insignificance. To paraphrase a tradition from Buddhism's narrative, resolving the doctrinal divisions between Buddhism and Christianity "is not conducive to awakening," because issues of social and environmental justice are not religion specific and neither are the solutions to these issues.

Therefore, the real question is, from what do persons need liberation? Persons need liberation from poverty, political oppression, and violence;

from the dangers of the current ecological crisis that is bringing suffering to all sentient beings on Planet Earth, all of which have their roots in the dominant economic philosophy of this planet: market capitalism and its resulting consumerism. This is why Buddhists and Christians need to share each other's visions in our collective human struggle "for the common good"[40] of all beings, not just human beings. For all sentient beings are interdependently related, not just "Christian" or "Buddhist" human beings, even if Buddhist and Christian narratives doctrinally describe universal interdependence differently.

ENDNOTES

[1] Masao Abe and John B. Cobb Jr., "Buddhist-Christian Dialogue: Past, Present, Future," *Buddhist-Christian Studies* 1 (1981) 24.

[2] Christopher S. Queen, "Introduction: A New Buddhism," in *Engaged Buddhism in the West*, ed. Christopher S. Queen (Boston: Wisdom, 2000) 23–24. Queen also makes this argument in "Introduction: The Shapes and Sources of Engaged Buddhism," in *Engaged Buddhism: Buddhist Liberation Movements in Asia*, ed. Christopher S. Queen and Sallie B. King (Albany: State University of New York Press, 1996) 4–16.

[3] Queen, "Introduction," 23.

[4] Patricia Hunt-Perry and Lyn Fine, "All Buddhism is Engaged: Thich Nhat Hanh and the Order of Interbeing," in *Engaged Buddhism in the West*, 35–62.

[5] John B. Cobb Jr., *Christ in a Pluralistic Age* (Philadelphia: Westminster, 1975) 206.

[6] See John B. Cobb Jr., *The Structure of Christian Existence* (Philadelphia: Westminster, 1972) 16–17 for his definition of "structure of existence."

[7] Cobb, *Christ in a Pluralistic Age*, 208–9.

[8] Ibid., 215–18. Abe also agrees with Cobb's assessment. See his conversation with Cobb in "Buddhist-Christian Dialogue," 13–29.

[9] See my fuller critique of Cobb's dialogue with Buddhism in "To John Cobb: Questions to Gladden the Atman in an Age of Pluralism," *JAAR* Supplement (June 1977) L753–88.

[10] George Dreyfus. "Meditation as Ethical Activity," *Journal of Buddhist Ethics* 2 (1995) 31–34 [Online]. Available FTP: ftp.cac.psu.edu Directory: JBE2/1995 File: dreyfus.txt.

[11] Winston L. King, "Engaged Buddhism: Past, Present, Future," *The Eastern Buddhist* (Autumn 1994) 14.

[12] Thich Naht Hanh, *Lotus in a Sea of Fire* (London: SCM, 1961).

[13] See Thich Naht Hanh, *Being Peace* (Berkeley: Parallax, 1988); idem, *The Heart of Understanding: Commentaries on the Prajñaparamita Sutra* (Berkeley: Parallax, 1988).

[14] This conclusion is argued rather well by King, "Engaged Buddhism," 14–29. I will not repeat his arguments.

[15] Charles S. Prebish, "Text and Tradition in the Study of Buddhist Ethics," *Pacific World* 9 (1993) 49–68.

[16] See Phra Rajavaramuni, "Foundations of Buddhist Social Ethics," in *Ethics, Wealth, and Salvation: A Study of Buddhist Social Ethics*, ed. Russell F. Sizemore and Donald K. Swearer (Columbia: University of South Carolina Press, 1992) 29–40.

[17] See, for example, Damien Keown, "Are There Human Rights in Buddhism?" *Journal of Buddhist Ethics* 2 (1995) 3–27 [Online]. Available FTP: ftp.cac.psu.edu Directory: JBE\21995 File: Keown.text. See Dreyfus for a friendly critique of Keown's specific application of virtue ethics to Buddhist ethics, especially the Western notion of "human rights."

[18] See Winston L. King, *In the Hope of Nibbana* (La Salle: Open Court, 1964) 203.

[19] Rajavaramuni, "Foundations of Buddhist Ethics," 46–53.

[20] Frank E. Reynolds, "Ethics and Wealth in Theravada Buddhism," in *Ethics, Wealth, and Salvation: A Study of Buddhist Social Ethics*, 50–76. See also David Little's response to Reynolds in "Ethical Analysis and Wealth in Theravada Buddhism: A Response to Frank Reynolds," in ibid., 77–86.

[21] John S. Strong, ed., *The Experience of Buddhism: Sources and Interpretations* (Belmont, Calif.: Wadsworth, 1995) 162–63.

[22] Robert A. F. Thurman, trans., *The Holy Teaching of Vimalakīrti* (University Park: Pennsylvania State University Press, 1976) 20, cited in King, "Engaged Buddhism" 17.

[23] King, 22–23. See also Harold D. Lasswell and Harlan Cleveland, eds., *The Ethic of Power* (New York: Harper and Row, 1992) 53.

[24] Donald K. Swearer, *Buddhism and Society in South East Asia* (Chambersburg, Pa.: Anima, 1980) 59–69. See also Swearer, ed., *Me and Mine: Selected Essays of Bhikkhu Buddhadasa* (Albany: State University of New York Press, 1989) chapters 10–12 and Sulak Sivaraksa, *A Socially Engaged Buddhism* (Bangkok: The Interreligious Commission for Development, 1988).

[25] See Kenneth K. S. Ch'an, *Buddhism in China: A Historical Survey* (Princeton, N.J.: Princeton University Press, 1979) chapter 16.

[26] Henrich Dumoulin and John C. Maraldo, eds., *Buddhism in the Modern World* (New York: Macmillan, 1976) chapter 16.

[27] Ibid., chapter 17.

[28] The best description of Vietnamese Buddhist social engagement prior to the end of the Vietnam War is still Jerrold Schecter's *The New Face of Buddha* (Tokyo: Weatherhill, 1967) chapters 8–11.

[29] See Bonkin Kim, "The Irwon Symbol and its Ecumenical Significance," *Buddhist-Christian Studies* 14 (1994) 73–87.

[30] See David W. Chappell, "Racial Diversity in the Soka Gakkai," in *Engaged Buddhism in the West*," 184–219; and idem, "Socially Inclusive Buddhists in America," *Global Citizens: The Soka Gakkai Buddhist Movement in America*, ed. David Machacek and Bryan Wilson (Oxford: Oxford University Press, 2000) 299–325. See also Jane Hurst, "Nichiren Shoshu and Soka Gakkai in America: The Pioneer Spirit," in *The Faces of Buddhism in America*, ed. Charles S. Prebish and Kenneth K. Tanaka (Berkeley: University of California Press, 1998) 49–78.

[31] The clearest description of the principles of Buddhist non-violent social activism is Sallie B. King's concluding essay, "Conclusion: Buddhist Social Activism," in Queen and King, ed., *Engaged Buddhism: Buddhist Liberation Movements in Asia*, 401–35.

[32] Kenneth Kraft, ed., *Inner Peace, World Peace: Essays on Buddhism and Nonviolence* (Albany: SUNY Press, 1992).

[33] Ibid., 12.

[34] Ibid.

[35] His Holiness Tenzen Guatso, *Kindness, Clarity, and Insight* (Ithaca, N.Y.: Snow Lion, 1984) 56–64; and idem, *The Way to Freedom* (San Francisco: HarperSanFrancisco, 1994) 58–64.

[36] Cited in King, "Engaged Buddhism," 24.

[37] However, contemporary Catholic ethical theory, rooted in the theology of Thomas Aquinas, whose ethical thought was in turn grounded in Aristotle's ethics, has engendered Catholic understanding of, and deep appreciation for, Buddhist social engagement. For an excellent discussion of the differences between Protestant and Roman Catholic ethics, see James M. Gustafson, *Protestant and Roman Catholic Ethics: Prospects for Rapprochement* (Chicago: University of Chicago Press, 1978). Also see Etienne Gilson, *The Christian Philosophy of St. Thomas Aquinas* (New York: Random House, 1956) 251–356.

[38] See John P. Keenan, "Some Questions About the World," in *The Sound of Liberating Truth: Buddhist-Christian Dialogues in Honor of Frederick J. Streng*, ed. Sallie B. King and Paul O. Ingram (Surrey: Curzon, 1999) 181–85.

[39] John Dominic Crossan, *The Dark Interval: Toward a Theology of Story* (Sonoma, Calif.: Polebridge, 1988) 101–7; also cited by Keenan, "Some Questions About the World," 183.

[40] Herman E. Daly and John B. Cobb Jr., *For the Common Good: Redirecting the Economy toward Community, the Environment, and a Sustainable Future*, 2d ed. (Boston: Beacon, 1994).

Chapter 5

On Buddhist-Christian Dialogue with the Natural Sciences

As I have noted, the thesis that has emerged from my particular wrestling match with God is that the two most important tasks of Christian theological reflection are (1) conceptual, socially engaged, and interior dialogue with the world's religions; and (2) contextualzing the practice of interreligious dialogue by what the natural sciences are discovering about the physical processes structuring the universe.[1] This chapter is about the patterns of Christian and Buddhist conceptual dialogue with the natural sciences. While Buddhists and Christians do not interact with the natural sciences in identical ways, including the sciences as a third partner in Buddhist-Christian conceptual encounter should engender new opportunities for mutual creative transformation.

Ian Barbour identifies five features of contemporary scientific developments that constitute a challenge, not only to Christian tradition, but to all religious traditions: the success of the methods of scientific investigation; the differences between scientific cosmologies and traditional religious cosmologies; the new contexts that science provides for theological reflection on religious understandings of human nature, particularly the doctrine of creation in the monotheistic religions; the fact of religious pluralism, which calls into question exclusive claims for any one religious tradition; and global threats to the environment and the subsequent necessity for religious people to turn toward science to understand the ecological interdependence of all life forms.[2]

It seems clear that what the natural sciences are revealing about the universe have become epistemological models for other disciplines of inquiry. The sciences appear to give us real knowledge of the physical structure of the universe because scientific theories and laws bear some resemblance to the actualities of the universe they describe, that is, they have ontological reference to physical reality.[3] But as John Cobb warns, human beings cannot live by scientific abstractions alone, because patterns of scientific abstractions cannot tell us how to constitute ourselves in community with each other and with other sentient life forms with whom we share this planet.[4]

It is also clear that scientific theories cannot be taken as literal descriptions of the physical universe, as classical realism assumed. Nor are scientific theories merely calculating devices whose only function is to allow the correlation and prediction of experimental observations, as instrumentalism holds. Most working scientists hold a middle position between classical realism and instrumentalism that Barbour calls "critical realism": scientific theories and models are "abstract symbol systems, which inadequately and selectively represent particular physical aspects of the world for specific purposes."[5] Critical realism thereby points to a working scientist's real intention while recognizing that scientific theories and models are imaginative human constructs intended to bear ontological correspondence to reality; they are neither literal pictures nor useful fictions, but limited and revisable ways of imagining what the physical structures of the universe are.

Second, in agreement with John Polkinghorne, as well as Barbour's description of critical realism, I want to make a similar claim for theological models. As successful scientific models and theories have broad explanatory power because they make physical processes intelligible (because they have ontological reference to reality), so too should theological models be expected to have broad explanatory power (because they too have ontological reference to reality). Like scientific models, theological models should make coherent sense of broad areas of experience because they bear some relation to the actuality of the world. Scientific theories may refer to unseeable entities (quarks and gluons) and theological models to an invisible God, yet the warrant for belief in the existence of these entities is that the structure of existence provides a basis for understanding what is happening. According to the "weak" version of the "anthropic principle," this is so because the structure of human minds that imperfectly understand these processes and structures are themselves interdependent with the evolutionary processes and structures human minds understand.[6] Accordingly, scientists and theologians should share a common commitment: truth exists to be found, or more accurately, approximated, whether or not it is actually found or approximated.

Of course the analogies between scientific method and theological method and between scientific theory and theological theory are not complete. The objects of theological knowledge and scientific knowledge are not identical; nor are the functions of scientific models and theories identical to those of theological models and theories—which does not imply that the natural sciences and theology are incommensurable fields of inquiry. But differences are important and should not be discounted. Theological reflection does not have the luxury of experimentation with controllable and repeatable bits of experience. The closest scientific analogues to theology are cosmology's reconstruction of the history of the universe's evolution immediately following the Big Bang and biology's interpretation of the fossil record of the history of the evolutionary development of life on Earth.

Third, scientific and theological insights demand response and carry ethical implications for human action. Because both science and theology are concerned with the question of truth and how persons should live in accord with truth, neither science nor theology can be ethically neutral. Nor will either discipline ever attain a total grasp of reality. Yet for both disciplines there is reasonable hope for developing approximate understandings of reality.

Finally, some writers think the sciences have discovered a common origin narrative that tells us how the universe evolved and how it works that can provide most of the world's religious traditions with a common origins myth. As Polkinghorne argues from his perspective as a physicist, there is no a priori reason that scientific theories and models and beautiful equations should prove to be the clue to understanding nature; why fundamental physics should be possible; why our minds should have such ready access to the deep structure of the universe. It is a contingent fact that this is true of us and of our world, but it does not seem sufficient simply to regard it as a happy accident. Surely it is a significant insight into the nature of reality.

As a Christian theologian, Polkinghorne concludes:

> I believe that Dirac and Einstein, making their great discoveries, were participating in an encounter with the divine. . . . There is much more to the Mind of God than physics will ever disclose, but this usage is not misleading, for I believe that the rational beauty of the cosmos reflects the Mind that brings it into being. . . . I do not present this conclusion as a logical demonstration—we are in a realm of metaphysical discourse where such certainty is not available either to believer or unbeliever—but I do present it as a coherent and intellectually satisfying understanding[7]

While Polkinghorne does not explicitly assert that scientific models, theories, or methods are proper epistemological models for all forms of inquiry, he does suggest that a common origin story is now emerging among contemporary physicists, biologists, and cosmologists that in broad outline confirms what the creation stories of many of the world's religions tell us about what the universe is and how we should live in it. In other words, the scientific story of the universe provides a common hermeneutical framework that links together a variety of religious creation stories. Brian Swimme, who is also a physicist, continues Polkinghorne's thought further:

> Precisely because this story of the universe comes to us through our investigations beginning with our eyes and ears and body we can speak of a transcultural creation story. Members of every continent are involved in discovering and articulating this story. Members of every religious tradition are involved in its telling.[8]

In broad strokes, this common origin story claims that some twelve to fourteen billion years ago the universe began from an explosion of matter that was infinitely small, infinitely hot, and infinitely concentrated outward to create some hundred billion galaxies, including our galaxy, the Milky Way, which itself contains billions of stars and our sun and its planets. All things that have lived, now live, and will ever live are the evolutionary effects of this primal "big bang" and its evolutionary history. Therefore, all things and events that ever have been, now are, or ever will be, are interrelated and interdependent from the very beginning. We are relatives of the stars, the oceans, the earth, and all creatures that have lived, now live, or will live. The entire universe is interrelated and organic in structure, a dynamic reality, constantly moving and becoming, always in process. This implies that the universe is radically open ended: creative of ever new novelty, things and events never before imagined yet always coming-to-be in interdependence with what went on before—ideas that should bring a smile of recognition to Buddhists and Christian process theologians.

While Swimme does not think that scientific cosmology can simply replace the basic content of religious creation myths, he does think that scientific cosmology can clarify and transform religious creation myths. As any lived myth does, scientific cosmology gives expression to religious experiences and convictions that are already present in all religious communities; it is a common origin story that is available to be re-mythologized by most religious traditions in terms of their own specific histories and practices. Accordingly, scientific cosmology is a place of meeting for the world's religions. Furthermore, our common story of the universe—with its revelation of universal interdependence and interrelationship—provides us with a means for breaking the road blocks that many post-modern thinkers put up before any universal ethical venture or truth claim. To the post-modern insistence—itself a universal truth claim that is, when pushed to its logical conclusion, incoherent with its own assumptions—that every theological and religious claim based on universal criteria is nothing but a social construction of the politically powerful, valid only for its own backyard, we can hold up a common story of the universe that tells us that all things are interrelated and interdependent.

In asserting that scientific cosmology provides us with a "metadiscourse" of the universe by which it is possible to link individual discourses—such as theology, ethics, or politics, or the teachings and practices of different religious traditions—Swimme does claim that scientific conclusions provide universal criteria for judging all truth claims, or that truth claims can be neatly and easily articulated by means of interreligious dialogue with the natural sciences. Furthermore, it is wise not to dismiss uncritically the specter of post-modernism's most important warning. As it is always dangerous to identify what is common in human experience in general, it is equally dangerous to identify what is common in humanity's religious experience in particular. Yet we are not condemned to the debilitating relativism that post-modernists tell us is ingredient in the personal or communal construction of perspectives from which we are free to make any selection we wish as we shop through the history of ideas. As the Buddhist deconstructionist Nagarjuna taught in India in the second century BC, there is always a middle way between certainty and relativism, which I think corresponds to critical realism's advice that we adhere to rational beliefs held with conviction but open to the likelihood of correction.

But there is a hiccup. As a Lutheran historian of religion, I am more sure of the theological challenges and contributions of dialogue with the natural science for Christian faith and practice than I am of the contributions dialogue with the sciences might make to Buddhist faith and practice. It's not just that Buddhists need to decide this matter for themselves. Buddhists who write about the natural sciences seem agreed that the structure of Buddhist doctrine and practice is supported rather than challenged by the natural sciences. That is, scientific theory seems to have had little effect, positive or negative, on Buddhism's worldview, doctrines, or practices. Accordingly, Buddhism may be evidence against Swimme's thesis that current scientific cosmology provides a common origin story most religious traditions can remythologize in terms of their distinctive creation myths.

Since Christian monotheism and Buddhist non-theism seem so incommensurable, reflection on the current scientific origin story that both Christians and Buddhists now share will serve as an illustration of my dilemma. According to this story, twelve to fourteen billion years ago the contents of the universe were together in an initial singularity, meaning a region of infinite curvature and energy density at which the known laws of physics break down.[9] There was a Big Bang. Distant galaxies of stars are even today receding in the aftermath of that violent explosive singularity.

The Big Bang was surely a cataclysmic event, and it is natural to suppose that it marked the origin of the universe and that every thing and event that has existed, exists now, or will exist is the result of this explosion. This being so, it seems reasonable to ask what caused the Big Bang.

The traditional Christian—and Jewish and Islamic—answer is to affirm that God created the universe. But there is a problem with the Christian view of creation: cosmologists claim that the Big Bang marked not only the coming into existence of the contents of the universe, but also the start of time. There was not time before the Big Bang, so there can be no cause of the Big Bang. "What place then for a creator?" asks Stephen Hawking in *A Brief History of Time,*[10] to which one might add, "or divine agency in the continuing processes of nature?"

The Buddhist answer to Hawking's question is that there is no place for a creator or for divine agency. Non-theism has always been the center of the Buddhist worldview so that Buddhists like Geoffrey Redmond argue that contemporary cosmology readily harmonizes with Buddhism. He writes:

> Buddhism does have a cosmology which differs considerably from that of Western science but its nature is such that it can be considered as a metaphor without weakening the Buddhist edifice. Cosmology never had the centrality that creation has in the Judeo-Christian tradition. Buddhism never committed itself to a particular ontology of its divine elements which could be contradicted by modern psychological or anthropological conceptions of such beliefs as metaphorical or archetypal.[11]

"By this analysis," Redmond continues, "Buddhism is closer to science than is revealed religion in the way it seeks truth."[12]

A more strident statement of this conclusion—one held in one form or another by many Western Buddhists—is that of B. Alan Wallace:

> As science continues to develop . . . it appears to enter into increasing conflict with the doctrines of Judaism and Christianity . . . . Contemporary views of geology, evolution, and cosmology repudiate biblical accounts of the origins of the earth, life, and the cosmos. Physics provides no coherent way of viewing the miracles reported in the Bible,

and neuroscience finds no place for the Christian concept of the human soul. What science does is leave us with a vast, impermanent universe consisting of matter and energy, in which life and consciousness occurred by accident.[13]

Of course, the challenge to the Christian doctrine of creation is crystal clear. One way theologians in dialogue with the sciences have responded is by reflecting on the relation between space and time in the scientific creation story. As I as understand this story, the Big Bang was an unusual explosion because it did not take place at a particular location or time in space. This means there existed no space outside the Big Bang. A common analogy to imagine this conclusion is a rubber balloon onto which are glued a number of coins. The coins represent galaxies. As air is pumped into the balloon, it expands. Suppose a fly were to land on one of the coins. What would it see? All the other coins moving away from it, which is, of course, the observed motion of the galaxies relative to scientists observing them from the Earth.

Astronomers now interpret the motion of the galaxies as being due to the space between galaxies expanding, rather than the galaxies moving through space. In other words, the galaxies are being carried outward from the singularity of the Big Bang on a tide of expanding space, just as coins glued to a balloon are carried apart by its rubber as the balloon expands. Furthermore, just as there is no empty stretch of rubber surface "outside" the region where the coins are glued, so there is no empty three-dimensional space outside where galaxies are to be found. It is this interpretation of the recession of the galaxies that leads cosmologists to conclude that all space that now exists was squashed to an infinitesimal singularity at the Big Bang. In other words, space began as nothing and has continued to expand ever since.

There is also an even more extraordinary element of this cosmology. According to Einstein's theory of general relativity, space and time are welded together as a four-dimensional continuum called "space-time." One cannot have space without time or time without space. In Buddhist language, they are "co-originated," meaning "interdependent." This being so, the Big Bang marked not only the coming into existence of space, but also the existence of time. This means that as there is no space before the Big Bang, there is also no time before the Big Bang, which in turn means that the "origin point" of the Big Bang is everywhere, so that the Big Bang occurred everywhere and is expanding into itself.

It is this aspect of contemporary scientific cosmology that many Buddhists believe gets rid of the sort of creator God that most people have in mind when they think of the Genesis creation story: a God who first exists alone and then at some point in time decides to create the universe. God says some words, there is a Big Bang, and WHAM, creation begins. Indeed, if the word God refers to this sort of entity, Buddhist non-theism seems more closely allied with current scientific cosmology than Christian monotheism.

However, much depends, as physicist Russell Stannard notes, on the meaning of the word "God." Consider the following quotation from St. Augustine:

> It is idle to look for time before creation, as if time can be found before time. If there were no motion of either a spiritual or corporal creature by which the future, moving through the present, would succeed the past, there would be no time at all. We should therefore say that time began with creation, rather than creation began with time.[14]

In other words, for God, there is neither before nor after; God simply *is* in a motionless eternity. Time and space are part of creation. Before creation, there is neither time nor space, and therefore literally "no-thing."[15] Deeply influenced by Platonic ideas, Augustine could write as early as his *Confessions*: "It is not in time that you [God] precede all times; all your 'years' subsist in simultaneity, because they do not change; your 'years' are 'one day' and your today is eternity.[16]

Stannard thinks contemporary cosmologists find it difficult to come to terms with Augustine's view of the beginning of time:

> If the archaic expression "either a spiritual or corporeal creature" had been replaced by a more up-to-date one, such as "a physical object," one might well have thought that the quote came from Hawking or some modern cosmologist. . . . It was a theologian who got there before them, by 1500 years.[17]

Here's how. We know time exists because things change—in Buddhist language, all things change because all things are impermanent. If nothing changed, if nothing "moved," in Augustine's language, we could not distinguish one point in time from another and there would be no way of determining to what the word "time" referred. Accordingly, Augustine argued, if there were no objects that change, that is, "move," there would be no objects at all. "Time" would be a meaningless category. Further, if there is no time, there is no space ("either") for objects to move through or occupy. In other words, no moving objects, no time; no time, no space.[18]

So, Augustine deduced, time and space are as much a property of the created universe as anything else and it makes no sense to think of God predating the creation of the universe. Yet none of this had an adverse effect on Augustine's theology because he noted that there is an important distinction between the words "creation" and "origins."[19] While in everyday conversations we might use these words interchangeably, in Christian theological discourse since Augustine each word has its own distinctive meanings. For example, if one has in mind a question like "How did the universe begin?" one is asking a question of origins. Questions of origins are matters for scientists to decide, their current research pointing to the Big Bang cosmology.

The question of "creation" is different from the question of "origins." The question of the origins of the universe has to do with what started the processes that ended up as the universe. This is essentially a descriptive and empirical issue. But the question of creation is a metaphysical issue, not a scientific one: "Why is there something and not nothing?" Creation, therefore, has as much to do with the present instant of time as any other instant of time. Why are we here? To whom or to what do we owe our existence? What keeps us in existence? The question of creation concerns the underlying "ground" of all things and events in space-time, past, present, and future.

Accordingly, when most Christian theologians write about God the Creator, they usually couple this with the idea of God's continual creation. God's creativity is not just invested in the first instant of time, but is also distributed throughout all subsequent time thereafter. Every thing and event that exists is not merely the end result of some instantaneous action of God twelve to fourteen billion years ago that set in causal sequence all the events that have happened subsequently, requiring no further attention from God—the deist error. Christian faith is not about a God who slaps the universe together like a mechanic welding the parts of a car and then moves on without further involvement after the job is done.

My own tentative conclusions in this matter involve certain Whiteheadian cosmological speculations in light of Big Bang cosmology. The usual interpretation of the Big Bang singularity is that it was the origin of space (and time) in every sense. But Alfred North Whitehead thought there can the be no pre-existent empty space so there could never be a time when there was no time.[20] It is this that made it so difficult to fit Whitehead's conceptuality into contemporary scientific cosmology. But some process writers think matters are not as difficult as many have thought. While the Big Bang is the origin of matter, some physicists speak of a "superspace" in which the Big Bang occurred and in which there exist other universes occupying this superspace at great distances. If so, the Big Bang is the origin of our universe in a previously empty "region" of super-space.

Of course, much depends on the meaning of "emptiness." For physicists, space contains a great deal of energy in the form of "virtual particles." For Whitehead, it is a plenum of actual occasions. The space is "empty" because these occasions are not related in a way that constitutes enduring objects, i.e., galaxies, stars, solar systems, and planets. These "virtual particles" or actual occasions are not discernible by means of current scientific instruments, although apparently their effects on our universe have been detected. The emergence of enduring objects (galaxies, stars, solar systems, planets, us) is an enormous change, and it can be called either "creation out of nothing" or "order out of chaos," since the actual occasions in empty space (virtual particles) are without order. Furthermore, this idea does not engender metaphysical problems of the sort suggested by extreme forms of the idea of creation out of nothing. If nothing means "no thing" and the "things" in question are enduring objects, then the language is acceptable, but each actual occasion, as well as the universe itself, comes into being out of antecedent actual occasions (virtual particles).

According to Rem B. Edwards[21] and Ervin Laszlo, theistic under-standings of Big Bang cosmology seem like a reasonable hypothesis, even if many physicists disagree. They suggest in their own ways that the order found in our universe is so remarkable that those wishing to avoid theism have tried to develop truly extraordinary speculations. Laszlo proposes a succession of universes in which the knowledge gained in each is preserved in empty space and directs later universes more wisely.[22] Edwards reports that many cosmologists posit innumerable unrelated universes scattered through superspace.[23] The only reason for such speculations is to show that the features of the universe we inhabit can be explained as a matter of chance: if there are millions of universes, the fact that the order in our universe has a probability of only one in many millions does not count against its chance character.

Of course, there is no evidence for or against theories of multiple universes. Furthermore, there is nothing in Whitehead's conceptuality to discourage such speculations. Nevertheless, a cosmic intelligence can account for the remarkable order of the universe we inhabit more easily than theories of multiple universes. If there were evidence that no such intelligence exists, or no evidence in its favor, then there would be rational grounds for affirming theories of multiple universes, of which our universe originated purely by chance. But since the ongoing course of events and some forms of religious experience do give some independent reasons for supposing the existence of a creator, which some religious traditions name "God," theistic speculation seems to have some advantages over non-theistic interpretations.[24]

Just how the emergence of order among actual occasions in "empty" space occurred remains mysterious at this time. It is for physicists to give us further clarification, if they can. But it now seems like the Big Bang singularity from which our universe emerged set off the release of enormous energy and brought an infinitely expanding universe into being. I have no doubt that physicists will discover new and amazing information about the universe. But I think it unlikely that there will be evidence against the hypothesis that "empty" space preceded the Big Bang. In fact, it seems more reasonable to assume that this empty space was a plenum of actual occasions or "virtual particles," that a primal decision established the constants in the universe (like the speed of light), and that God has lured all creatures toward actualizations of greater value made possible, but not necessitated by, the Big Bang.

The usual Buddhist response to these notions is to dismiss the question of the universe's creation as a meaningless concept, since traditional

Buddhist cosmology describes the universe as an eternally changing system of interdependent interrelationships without beginning or end. Contemporary Western Buddhists, especially, think we should simply accept the universe as a brute fact. They ask what, if anything, is gained by affirming that God created it. For Buddhists, the Christian doctrine of creation, even in Whiteheadian understandings, not only raises the question of who created God; it also implies that any notion of divine creation encourages clinging (*taṇhā*) to an imagined permanent sacred reality. The karmic result of such clinging to imagined permanent realities can only be suffering (*duḥkha*).[25]

From a mainline Christian point of view, however, Buddhist criticism of Christian notions of creation misrepresents how Christian theology uses the word "God." Paul Tillich appropriated Augustine's notions of time when he wrote that God is not an existent object or "being."[26] In other words, one cannot say that God "exists" in the same way that one can say "apples exist," or for that matter, "the universe exists." The point of the Christian doctrine of creation is that God is the source of all existence; "God" is the name Christians (and Jews and Muslims) give to whatever is responsible for the existence of all space-time things and events, including human beings. So the trouble with most Buddhist interpretations of the Christian doctrine of creation is that they mistakenly assume that Christians affirm God as an object confined within the limits of space and time or that God can only exist "in time." Certainly, one hears such theological talk among Christians. But the mainline teaching is that, while we experience God in time and space, God is not confined by time and space. Process theology especially stresses that everything is in continual mutual interaction with God in time (God's consequent nature).[27] But God in God's primordial nature is also "beyond" time (and space), meaning God transcends time (and space) primordially even as God is immanent consequently in time (and space).

None of the challenges posed to the themes of traditional Christian theism—God as creator, both "in the beginning" and continually in the present—seemingly pose any challenge to Buddhism's non-theistic worldview. If this is really the case, how can Buddhist faith and practice be creatively transformed by conceptual dialogue with Christian theology mediated by the sciences as a "third party" in the dialogue? Reflection on this question will require a brief description of the sorts of conversations with the sciences Buddhists are now undertaking.

While typologies are always dangerous because they run the risk of what Whitehead called "the fallacy of misplaced concreteness," they are often heuristically helpful. In his typology of the ways scientists and Christian theologians have tried to relate science and religion, Barbour describes four models: (1) conflict, (2) independence, (3) dialogue, and (4) integration.[28] Identifying how these options have operated in Christian reflection should clarify the differences between Christian and Buddhist encounter with the natural sciences. Following this, I will offer some conclusions in process about how dialogue with the natural sciences might be included in current Buddhist-Christian encounter.

The conflict model assumes that science and religion are by nature opposed and necessarily in conflict. Scientific materialism, sometimes characterized as "scientism," is an example of this model. Materialists tend to assume that scientific method is the only reliable source of knowledge and that everything that can be known is reducible to the interaction between physical forces and is mathematically explainable only in terms of these forces. Accordingly, religious doctrines in conflict with science are illusory and bear no correspondence to reality.

The opposite of scientific materialism is "creation science" based on Biblical literalism. Scientific descriptions of natural processes in conflict with the Bible are treated as illusory and bear no correspondence to the way God created the universe and guides its history. Both scientism and creation science, as well as "intelligent design" and other examples of the conflict model, err in assuming that scientific theory is inherently atheistic, and thereby they both perpetuate the false dilemma of having to choose between religion and science. Since the conflict model is inherently non-dialogical, it cannot contribute to either Buddhist or Christian dialogue with the natural sciences.

The independence model asserts that science and theology are totally independent and autonomous enterprises. Each should keep off the other's turf and tend to its own specific concerns and not meddle in the affairs of the other. Since both fields of inquiry are selective and have their own limitations, each is separated into watertight compartments. This epistemological dualism is motivated not only by the desire to avoid conflict, but also to remain faithful to the specific character of scientific and theological disciplines. Theology and science are different "languages" that are unrelated because their "objects of discourse" are unrelated. Examples of this approach include Protestant Neo-Orthodoxy, particularly the theology of Karl Barth, theological existentialism exemplified by Paul Tillich, Martin Buber, Rudolf Bultmann, Langdon Gilkey, and Thomas Torrance, as well as theologians influenced by Wittgenstein's philosophy. Another theologian in this category is George Lindbeck, who asserts that theology and science are different "language games" whose functions are not reducible to one another.

The independence model has several drawbacks. Protestant Neo-Orthodoxy, in most of its variations, asserts that revelation and salvation occur only in Christ, which seems theologically problematic given the realities of religious pluralism. Theological Existentialism tends to privatize religious experience to the neglect of its communal dimensions. If God acts exclusively in the realm of selfhood and not in the realm of nature, as Barth (who was not a theological existentialist) and Buber and Bultmann believed, the natural order is devoid of religious significance. If theology deals with the self and science with nature, there is no need to say anything about the relation between science and religion because no relation exists. There can be no dialogue between separate realms of discourse.

The dialogue model maintains that theology and science are separate disciplines concerned with different objects of inquiry; each employing different methodologies that are appropriate to their fields of inquiry. Dialogue starts from general theories of science and nature as means of apprehending ways of contextualzing theology by relating it to what the sciences are telling us about the structure of physical reality. Wolfhart Pannenberg is a proponent of this model.

The integration model holds that some sort of integration between the actual content of science and the actual content of theology is a possibility. Here, the relations between specific scientific theories—for example, Big Bang cosmology—and specific theological doctrines—for example, the doctrine of creation—are more direct than in the dialogue model. There are three distinct versions of the integration model: (1) Natural Theology, exemplified by John Polkinghorne, which claims the existence of God can be inferred from the evidence of design in nature, of which science has made us more aware; (2) Theology of Nature, exemplified by Arthur Peacocke, in which the main sources of theology lie outside science, but scientific theories may affect the reformulation of certain doctrines, particularly the doctrines of creation and human nature; and (3) Systematic Synthesis, exemplified by Whiteheadian process theology, in which both science and theology contribute to developing an inclusive metaphysic.

With this typology in mind, we can now look at examples of Buddhist encounter with the natural sciences. For the most part, Buddhists have to this date stressed environmental ethics and psychology in their conversations with the natural sciences.[29] This assertion does not imply that Buddhists have paid no attention to physics and cosmology. But as in Christian theology, the focus of Buddhist interest in the natural sciences has stressed those areas where traditional Buddhist teachings might be supported by current scientific views of physical reality, in this case psychology and the biological sciences. Accordingly, Buddhist interest in ecology is closely linked to the Buddhist doctrine of dependent co-origination, which teaches that every thing and every event at every moment of space-time is co-created and constituted by the interdependently interpenetrating nexus of relationships it undergoes from moment to moment of its existence. While the notion of interdependence is affirmed by physicists and by cosmology, Buddhists have particularly focused on the biological interdependence affirmed by evolutionary theory. Likewise, Buddhist teachings about non-self (*anatta, anātman*) and the practice of meditation have led Buddhists to neurobiology and psychology as a means of translating their traditional doctrines of suffering and its causes (*duḥkha* and *taṇhā*), the meaning of "liberation" (*nirvāṇa*), and the practice of meditation into more contemporary contexts.

B. Alan Wallace, who writes about the relation between scientific theory and reality through the lenses of a practicing Tibetan Buddhist, will serve to illustrate both a Buddhist critique of physics and biology and Buddhist interest in psychology. In contrast to Polkinghorne, Wallace is highly critical of the principle of "critical realism" because he thinks scientific theories do not have ontological correspondence to physical realities.[30] Barbour's "independence model" best describes Wallace's thesis about the relation between science and Buddhism: while the sciences give us objective knowledge about physical processes, "they do not give us knowledge of an objective world." He writes:

> If we conclude that it [science] provides us with no ultimately reliable, objective knowledge, we may ask: what then, is the purpose of creating scientific theories? One response is that such theories do make natural events intelligible in their relation to our human existence. A second purpose is that they are extremely useful in learning to deal with natural events that have a strong bearing on our well-being. One facet of that purpose is the development of technology.[31]

Consequently, Wallace thinks the combined approaches of empirical scientific research and mathematical analysis give us "pragmatic truth" because they give us an enormous accumulation of information about the natural world. That is, scientific theories are "instrumental" and pragmatic because they "work." But as pragmatic truths about the physical world, scientific truths are "secondary truths," to employ Nagarjuna's two-truth theory, and in themselves shed little light on the meaning of human existence. Accordingly, "we err if we expect the natural sciences to solve issues of a metaphysical or religious nature, for it was never designed to probe such questions."[32] Metaphysical truth has to do with the absolute truth of Emptiness (*śūnyatā*). For Wallace, therefore, the primary weakness of physics and the biological sciences is that "neither discipline the mind and mental experience."[33] Buddhism, however, because of its strong empirical foundations and the deconstructive traditions of Madhyamika dialectics, can fill in this perceived weakness in Western physics and biology. He writes:

> At present, Western civilization has no cognitive science comparable to its physical sciences . . . Cognitive science in its present Western form investigates mental states objectively in the sense that the researcher performs tests on other people's mental functions. Since the researcher has no direct access to anyone else's mind, this approach treats the mind as a "black box." The information that is analyzed concerns input and output from the mind and senses, but cognition itself is not directly examined. This would entail a subjective perspective which is still regarded as unprofessional in today's scientific arena.[34]

Buddhism supplies this subjective perspective on cognitive processes, which is missing in contemporary neurophysiological and neuropsychological accounts of the origins of consciousness from non-conscious through biological processes.

Other Buddhists like Geoffrey Redmond argue that the Dharma seems to harmonize more readily with science than the other world religions because scientific notions of interdependence and other standard Buddhist doctrines seem parallel. In part, this is historical accident. Throughout most of Buddhism's history, there was no contact with the natural sciences. Buddhist encounter with the natural sciences began with sixteenth-century Western colonialism in East and South Asia. In this encounter, Buddhism does not appear to have felt the need to oppose Western science. Nor did the sciences challenge the fundamentals of Buddhism's worldview and doctrines in the way they challenged Christian theology. According to Redmond, this is because Buddhism is not committed to pre-scientific ideas so that Buddhism's traditional cosmology was never its essential core. Therefore, Buddhism was, and still is, less threatened by science than other world religions.[35] Even so, Redmond's view of the relation between Buddhism and the sciences is that they are independent enterprises.

Victor Mansfield takes Redmond's conclusion further. He argues that similarities between Madhyamika philosophy and modern physics in their understanding of time is evidence that Buddhism is particularly compatible with the natural sciences, especially in the area of neurobiology and psychology.[36] But compatibility with the natural sciences does not imply that Buddhism is "scientific." Both Redmond and Mansfield, as well as most Buddhists, think that asserting that Buddhism is "scientific" is a distortion of Buddhism. So while science is no threat to Buddhist teachings and practice, Buddhism has resources that can fill in the "gaps" of Western science relative to mental and emotional experiences and can help the psychological sciences develop coherent theories of cognition. In this way, in dialogue with Buddhism, science is more apt to be creatively transformed than is Buddhism through its dialogue with the sciences.

Shoyo Taniguchi goes beyond either Redmond or Mansfield and argues that Buddhism is scientific in a way other religions are not. She scrutinizes the Pali suttas and early Buddhist philosophy and pushes the interdependence model as far as it can probably go. She concludes that early Theravada Buddhism employs empirical and experimental methods equivalent to those of modern science and is therefore a "scientific" religion, meaning that Buddhist doctrines harmonize with current scientific models of physical reality in a way other religions do not.[37] Her tacit conclusion is that Buddhism is thereby superior to other religions, particularly Judaism, Christianity, and Islam because, in her view physics and evolutionary biology leave no room for a Creator.

It is clear that neither Wallace, Redmond, Mansfield, nor Taniguchi experience or interpret the natural sciences—particularly Big Bang cosmology and evolutionary Biology—as a challenge to Buddhist doctrine and practice. The distinct impression that Buddhist writing on the natural sciences seems to give is that the structure of Buddhist tradition remains untouched by the sciences, either positively or negatively.

Christian dialogue with the natural sciences has had the opposite effect on the structure of Christian thought and practice. Since Copernicus theorized that the planets revolve around the sun, which Galileo confirmed when he saw moons revolving around Jupiter through his telescope, no aspect of Christian doctrine has remained conceptually unchallenged by the natural sciences. I have already noted how current Big Bang cosmology has forced Christian theologians to rethink the doctrine of creation and the idea of God's continuing agency in the universe. Those debates continue. Evolutionary biology presents similar challenges to Christian theological conceptions.

This last point can be illustrated by Denis Edwards' reflection on the problem of evil in his book *The God of Evolution: A Trinitarian Theology*.[38] Edwards applies a version of the interdependence model in his view of the relation between science and theology. His working hypothesis is that science and faith are not separate languages. This is especially true of evolutionary theory, which he thinks provides actual knowledge about the way God works in nature to achieve divine purposes. "There is every reason," he writes, "for a Christian of today to embrace *both* the theological teachings of Genesis *and* the theory of evolution. But holding together the Christian view of God and the insights of evolutionary science does demand a rethinking of our theology of the Trinitarian God at work in creation."[39]

The God of evolution, for Edwards, is a trinitarian God interpreted panentheistically. In this he grounds his theology on Richard of St. Victor:

"The foundations for a theology that takes evolution seriously can be found in the trinitarian vision of God as a God of mutual relations, of a God who is communion in love, a God who is friendship beyond all comprehension."[40] One can immediately see the issue of theodocy in this attempt to integrate evolutionary biology into this vision of God. Evolutionary theory requires a long history of pain and suffering as sentient animals and entire species are ground up and spit out by the relentlessly impersonal process of natural selection. How can a God of love, friendship, and communion design a creation in which life must eat life for any species to survive, with the result that existence for all living things is replete with misery and death?

Edwards tries to deal with the theodocy problem in two ways. First, he tries to distinguish carefully between "suffering" and "pain." Natural selection is not cruel and animals do not suffer. To say that natural selection is cruel is to anthropomorphize nature by imparting human values to an impersonally operating process. For Edwards, nature—both theologically and scientifically understood—is impersonal and should not be understood anthropomorphically. Accordingly, by insisting that animals have pain but not suffering, Edwards reserves the term "suffering" for self-conscious human persons. So natural selection is not as cruel as we might think.

Edwards' second move is to affirm God's self-limitation in God's past and continual creation in nature. It is by self-limitation of the divine self that God makes creation possible. God's self-limitation also makes contingency and freedom, and thereby pain and suffering, possible, which in turn makes the self-creativity of creation possible—at a dreadful cost. The source of Edwards' understanding of God's self-emptying self is in the divine *kenosis* ("emptying") of the Cross, which he applies to the *kenosis* of creation in order to affirm God's self-shedding of omnipotence. In Edwards' words: "Omnipotence, understood in light of the cross, is the supreme power to freely give one's self in love. In light of this, the divine act of creation can be understood as an act of love, by which the trinitarian Persons freely make space for creation and freely accept the limits of the process."[41]

Of course, Christian theology, as well as Islamic philosophy and Jewish thought, has long wrestled with the question of the relation between human freedom and divine power. What Edwards does is slide this issue into evolutionary processes that include random mutations, natural selection, and evolutionary development. That is, Edwards thinks that by distancing the divine Self from creation, human beings can exercise freedom, and nature can be governed by randomness and chance. God, in creating the universe, accepts the limits of physical processes and of human freedom. Yet Edwards also affirms that God's purposes are also achieved through nature. His argument is that God should not be understood as another factor operating alongside natural selection, or in addition to it, but is rather to be understood as acting through it.

According to Ted Peters, Edwards' conclusions are incoherent because of the divine self-limitation argument itself:

> The difficulty here is not unique to Edwards. I find it emerging frequently in contemporary discussions of the relation of God to the world. Many theists whom I respect and revere—Langdon Gilkey, Jürgen Moltmann, Wolfhart Pannenberg, John Polkinghorne—are making the argument that impersonal contingency in nature and personal freedom in humanity require divine self-limitation, i.e., the absence of God rather than the presence of God. I tend to disagree, although I disagree respectfully.[42]

The fallacy in divine self-limitation arguments is that they presuppose a conflict between divine power and "creature power." Peters thinks the Christian teaching should emphasize that God's power empowers and thereby liberates God's creatures.

In his response to Peters, Edwards notes that the thrust of his argument is to contest any understanding of God's power as "almighty," meaning "the view that God can do absolutely anything without qualification."

> This view of divine power has never been that of the authentic theological tradition, which has always understood that God could never act in a way that is opposed to the divine nature, and this nature has always been understood as love. The view of divine power as dominating cannot be supported by Christology or trinitarian theology.[43]

If this is true, Edwards concludes, theologians need a different understanding of reality itself, a different metaphysics, a relational ontology that describes how the processes of nature really work. It is here that the sciences, in this case, evolutionary biology, reveal that the process of natural selection itself is interdependent, that is, relational. Theological notions that attribute absolute power to God are incapable of apprehending that reality is fundamentally relational and that even the laws that govern biological evolution originate from the creativity of God's "communion" with the world.

Debates like this between Edwards and Peters on how to understand foundational Christian doctrines in light of current scientific theory have not occurred as a result of Buddhist encounter with the natural sciences.

It's now time to bring this chapter to a conclusion and ask, "So what?" What, if anything, would Buddhist-Christian dialogue with the natural sciences add to current Buddhist-Christian encounter? While my conclusions are very much in process, I want to be crystal clear about what I am *not* arguing: (1) that Buddhism is deficient because the natural sciences have not challenged Buddhist doctrines in the same way that the natural sciences have challenged Christian doctrines; (2) that Christian tradition is "truer" or "superior" to Buddhist tradition because the natural sciences can be read as scientific confirmation of certain Christian doctrines, as, for example, in Polkinghorne's appropriation of the "weak" anthropic principle as an argument for the reasonableness of the doctrine of God as creator and sustainer of the universe; (3) that Buddhist dialogue with natural sciences should be modeled after Christian encounter with the natural sciences. I admire Buddhism and have been enriched by my dialogue with Buddhist tradition—through conceptual dialogue, socially engaged dialogue, and interior dialogue. But I am not a Buddhist, which means that I am in no position to positively or negatively judge the structure, forms, or conclusions of Buddhist dialogue with the natural sciences. What Buddhists receive through dialogue with the natural sciences is for Buddhists to decide. Consequently, what follows should be understood as descriptive and a bit tentative.

First, it is clear that Buddhists tend to read Big Bang cosmology and evolutionary theory as supportive of the Buddhist worldview. Buddhists do not seem to have experienced the natural sciences as a conceptual challenge. Nor have the sciences had much positive or negative effect on Buddhist meditative practices or on the devotional practices of Buddhism. Some Buddhist writers point to parallels between Buddhism's "non-theistic" worldview and current scientific cosmology as evidence that Buddhism is more in harmony with the sciences than Christian theism (Wallace, Redmond, and Mansfield). Some Buddhist writers take a stronger stance and affirm that scientific accounts of reality are proof of the superiority of Buddhism to all theistic religions (Taniguchi). Other Buddhists find Western psychology a "convenient means" or *upāya* for translating Buddhism's meditative practice into forms more accessible to Westerners, as well as for affirming that Buddhist meditation is "scientific" because its methods are "experimental" and "empirical" (Wallace).

Such arguments have a familiar ring. Nineteenth- and early-twentieth-century Western interpretations of Buddhism tended to see Buddhism as rational, experimental, empirical, and critical of authority beyond an individual's own experience—all treasured ideals of the Western Enlightenment. Yet Buddhists have not thought it necessary to rethink or reformulate the fundamental doctrines that shape Buddhism's structure of existence because of its conceptual encounter with the natural sciences. Those Buddhists writing from Mahayana Buddhist perspectives often apply Nagarjuna's two truths epistemology in their encounter with the sciences: scientific conclusions, models, paradigms, theories, and laws are identified as "secondary truths." The measure of the truth of scientific conclusions is "relative" and "pragmatic," meaning they "work," especially in the realm of technology. But the absolute truth, i.e., "Emptying" or *śūnyatā*, is absolutely beyond "discriminating mind" based on cause and effect relations, which themselves are "empty" of "self-existence" (*svabhāva*).[44] Such notions seem contrary to the "critical realism" assumed by most working scientists, for whom scientific theories and paradigms are not "secondary truths."

But there is a problem with those who, like Wallace and Mansfield, use Madhyamika dialects in their dialogue with the sciences. The problem begins when such a person claims that an opponent asserts proposition X, a proposition that the opponent is said to ascribe independent existence. The imagined opponent, perhaps a physicist, is unlikely to agree with this characterization. Nevertheless, such Buddhists typically go on to show the logical incoherence of X, thus reaffirming their own concept of emptiness. Sometimes such criticism of the opponent's view is legitimate, but often what is being criticized is a distortion of the opponent's view, with the result that neither side succeeds in deeply considering the other's position.

Misrepresenting how scientists actually understand their work is destructive of dialogue. A fruitful dialogue, on the other hand, assumes that each party has something to learn from the other and that the exchange can give deeper insight into individual commitments. Not that a scientist should necessarily become a Buddhist (or a Christian), or that a Buddhist should embrace science. But when there is one stock answer to all questions (that nothing really exists because everything's empty) then the exchange is predictable and infertile. Rather than refining, sharpening, and deepening Buddhism, we have philosophical isolation and inward turning that focuses on momentary bits of meditative experience. As beautiful and transformative as such inward turning can be, it is not conducive to dialogue with the natural sciences.

Second, Buddhism's conceptual encounter with the natural sciences parallels its conceptual dialogue with Christian theology. In conceptual dialogue with Christian theology, Buddhists have not experienced the same degree of creative transformation as have Christians in their dialogue with Buddhist philosophy—perhaps because Buddhism is more worldview specific than Christian tradition. Delete or redefine any of the doctrines implicit in Buddhism's worldview—non-self, impermanence, interdependence, non-theism—Buddhism ceases to be Buddhism. While theologians like John Cobb have even affirmed that "a Christian can be a Buddhist, too," provided that one is careful to explain what this means, no Buddhist writer in dialogue with Christian theology has yet written that "a Buddhist can be a Christian, too." So it would seem that Buddhists have concluded that conceptual dialogue with the natural sciences would contribute as little to Buddhism's creative transformation as its conceptual dialogue with Christian theology.

Nevertheless, Buddhists are as interested in the natural sciences as Christians, particularly in the practice of "socially engaged dialogue" with Christian traditions of social activism. Buddhists have learned much from Christian tradition (and *vice versa*) about confronting issues of oppression and injustice that are not religion specific: consumerism, gender issues, social justice issues, environmental issues, racism, war. The biological sciences have been particularly helpful to Buddhists and Christians in their socially engaged dialogue on environmental issues because these problems cannot be addressed apart from what evolutionary theory tells us about the structure of biological processes. Accordingly, a point of entry for Buddhist-Christian dialogue with the natural sciences is socially engaged dialogue.[45] Including the sciences as a third partner in socially engaged dialogue—especially the biological sciences and economics—would greatly empower current Buddhist and Christian cooperation in confronting justice and environmental issues.

Furthermore, the neurobiological sciences and psychology might make important contributions to the practice of Buddhist-Christian interior dialogue. The psychological dynamics and neurophysiological processes underlying disciplines like meditation and contemplative prayer, liturgical practices, and other forms of spirituality and community might shed light on Buddhist and Christian traditions of "practice," both in terms of similarities and differences of the experiences such practices engender. In this way, new information might be added to what is already known about Buddhist and Christian practice traditions.

My final conclusion in process is in the nature of a question. Is it really true that encountering the natural sciences poses no important conceptual challenges to Buddhism's worldview or to Buddhists doctrines? Consider the following:

My particular commitment to process theology notwithstanding, it is a fact that in the late twentieth century and now the twenty-first century, the displacement of God by Darwinian forces in scientific writing is almost complete.[46] Scientific writing, especially on evolution, shows this displacement clearly. In 1978, Edmond O. Wilson won the Pulitzer Prize for his book *On Human Nature*. Wilson's work on the social behavior of insects was widely admired as pioneering and led directly to his founding contributions to a new field that he called "social biology," defined as the study of the biological basis of social behavior. In the beginning of his book, Wilson clearly stated what he believed was the final displacement of God by Darwinian evolution: "If humankind evolved by Darwinian natural selection, genetic chance and environmental necessity, not God, made the species."[47] So much for the Christian doctrine of creation, scientists like Wilson declare. "No problem," Buddhists like Redmond believe, since Buddhist non-theism does not posit a doctrine of creation.

But watch what happens as the displacement of God by Darwinian evolution is pushed to its logical conclusions in scientific materialism.

Richard Dawkins agrees with Wilson and asserts that the Darwinian universe not only displaces God, it leaves no real place for values, for genuine good or evil. "This is one of the hardest lessons for humans to learn," he writes. "We cannot admit that things might be neither good nor evil, cruel nor kind, but simply callous—indifferent to all suffering, lacking all purpose."[48] Steven Weinberg draws the same conclusion from his work in reconstructing Big Bang cosmology: "The universe is pointless."[49]

First, Copernicus displaces humanity as the center of the universe. Then Big Bang cosmology and Darwinianism set aside God as the creator of the universe. And finally, according to this interpretation of the history of science, biochemistry and molecular biology remove all doubt that the properties of all living things can be explained in terms of, and reduced to, the physics and chemistry of ordinary matter. Everything is molecules.

The near-complete absence of religion from contemporary science is summarized, for me, by this description of the mating system of a species of monkeys, the Hanuman Langurs, in Northern India by George C. Williams, a scientist who has made important contributions to the understanding the complexities of natural selection.

> Their mating system is what biologists call harem polygyny: Dominant males have exclusive sexual access to a group of adult females, as long as they can keep other males away. Sooner or later, a stronger male usurps the harem and the defeated one must join the ranks of celibate outcasts. The new male shows his love for his new wives by trying to kill their unweaned infants. For each successful killing, a mother stops lactating and goes into estrous. . . . Deprived of her nursing baby, a female soon starts ovulating. She accepts the advances of her baby's murderer, and he becomes the father of her next child.
>
> *Do you still think that God is good?*[50]

So there it is. If the universe is pointless and meaningless, then what is the meaning of any religious tradition? Certainly, such conclusions are radically opposed to Christian notions of God and the whole edifice of Christian doctrine and practice. But these same views also contradict the whole edifice of Buddhism as well—if the scientific materialism of persons

93

like Wilson, Weinberg, Dawkins, and Williams are accurate descriptions of the way things really are in this universe.

Of course, the issue for Buddhism is not the "displacement of God." Nevertheless, the notion that all living things have evolved through accidental forces of random mutation and natural selection in the struggle for existence seems to raise as many questions regarding fundamental Buddhist doctrines as it does for Christian theology. Is the teaching that since all sentient beings are interdependent, we should experience the suffering of others as our suffering and act to relieve suffering by non-violent expedient means based on an illusion? In a universe that seems to demand suffering and death as the price for life itself, does it make any sense to say we cause our own suffering by clinging to impermanence and that we can free ourselves of suffering by training ourselves not to cling to permanence? Does universal suffering have anything to do with "clinging?" If the universe really is "pointless" and "without value," can Awakening mean anything more than becoming experientially aware of universal pointlessness? If the universe is valueless, what's the value of Awakening? Are compassion and non-violence merely fantasies? In a pointless and valueless universe, in what and for what can one reasonably hope? What is the connection between Buddhism's defining teachings and what the sciences are discovering about the physical processes of nature?

Only Buddhists can answer these questions. They are there to be answered whether or not Buddhists choose to confront them. Doing so in the context of conceptual dialogue with Christian theology and the natural sciences would, I believe, engender new forms of mutual creative transformation in both Buddhist and Christian tradition, as well as the natural sciences. Exactly how remains an open question, since the sciences have not as yet been included as dialogical partners in current Buddhist-Christian encounter. Perhaps it is time to start.

ENDNOTES

[1] Here, I am in agreement with John Polkinghorne: "The religious setting must be broadened beyond the Abrahamic faiths to include all religious traditions. It is suggested that their meeting with science may provide the world faiths with a congenial ground of encounter." *Belief in God in an Age of Science*, The Terry Lectures (New Haven: Yale University Press, 1998) xiii.

[2] Ian G. Barbour, *Religion and Science: Historical and Contemporary Issues* (San Francisco: HarperCollins, 1997) xii–xv.

[3] Ibid., 117–19.

[4] John B. Cobb Jr., "Global Theology in a Pluralistic Age," in *Transforming Christianity and the World*, ed. Paul F. Knitter (Maryknoll, N.Y.: Orbis, 1999) 53.

[5] Barbour, 117.

[6] The anthropic principle is a collection of scientific insights indicating that the possibility of carbon-based life depends on a very delicate balance among the forces of nature and (perhaps) also on very specific initial circumstances for the universe. In other words, the Universe seems "finely tuned" for human life so that the universe must be habitable by beings like us. The "weak" version of the anthropic principle adds that human understanding of the physical processes of the universe has ontological correspondence with physical reality because human minds are themselves the result of these processes. A "strong" version of the anthropic principle asserts that in the evolution of human beings, the universe itself has attained consciousness. I find the anthropocentric implication of the strong version troubling. From a scientific point of view, I doubt it can be argued that the culminating result of evolution is human self-consciousness. I also find the ethical implications of any form of anthropomorphism problematic, especially in relation to environmental issues. See Norriss S. Hetherington, *Cosmology: Historical, Literary, Philosophical, Religious, and Scientific Perspectives* (New York: Garland, 1993) 505–14.

[7] Polkinghorne, *Belief in God in an Age of Science*, 4–5.

[8] Brian Swimme, "Science: A Partner in Creating the Vision," *Thomas Berry and the New Cosmology*, ed. Anne Lonergan and Caroline Richards (Mystic, Conn.: Twenty-Third Publications, 1987) 86, also cited in Paul Knitter, *One Earth, Many Religions* (Maryknoll, N.Y.: Orbis, 1996) 120.

[9] See Jonathan J. Halliwell, "Quantum Cosmology and the Creation of the Universe," in *Cosmology: Historical, Literary, Philosophical, Religious, and Scientific Perspectives*, 477–97.

[10] Stephen W. Hawking, *A Brief History of Time* (New York: Bantam, 1988) 141.

[11] Geoffrey P. Redmond, "Comparing Science and Buddhism," *Pacific World* 11–12 (1995–96) 106.

[12] Ibid., 111.

[13] B. Alan Wallace, *Choosing Reality: A Buddhist View of Physics and the Mind* (Ithaca, N.Y.: Snow Lion, 1996) 10.

[14] *De Civitate Dei* (*The City of God*) XII.15, cited by Russell Stannard, "Where in the World is God?" *Research News and Opportunities in Science and Theology* 1 (October 2000) 13.

[15] See Etienne Gilson, *The Christian Philosophy of Saint Augustine* (New York: Random House, 1960) 190–91.

[16] Augustine, *Confessiones*, book 11; *Confessions* (Oxford: Oxford University Press, 1991) 230.

[17] Russell Stannard, "Where in the World is God?" 13.

[18] *De Civitate Dei* (*The City of God*) XII.15: "For where there is no creature whose changing movements admits to succession, there cannot be time at all." So also XI.6: "Time does

not exist without some movement and transition . . ." Also see Robert Jordan, "Time and Contingency in St. Augustine," in *Augustine: A Collection of Critical Essays*, ed. R. A. Markus (New York: Anchor, 1972) 255–79 and Hugh Lacy, "Empiricism and Augustine's Problem About Time," in ibid., 280–308.

[19] In what follows, I have relied on the following sources: Polkinghorne, *Belief in God in an Age of Science*, 1–12; idem, *The Faith of a Physicist* (Minneapolis: Fortress, 1996) chapter 4; Arthur Peacocke, *Theology for a Scientific Age* (Minneapolis: Fortress, 1993) 135–83; Mark William Worthing, *God, Creation, and Contemporary Physics* (Minneapolis: Fortress, 1996) 73–110; and Langdon Gilkey, *Nature, Reality, and the Sacred* (Minneapolis: Fortress, 1993) 161–204.

[20] Alfred North Whitehead, *Process and Reality* (New York: Macmillan, 1957) 108–119.

[21] Rem B. Edwards, "How Process Philosophy Can Affirm Creation *Ex Nihilo*," *Process Studies* 29 (Spring–Summer 2000) 77–98.

[22] See three unpublished manuscripts by Erwin Laszlo given at a conference at the Center for Process Studies, Claremont, California, in 2000. These manuscripts may be obtained by request from the Center for Process Thought [ctr4process.org] and are entitled: "The Theory of Psi Field: Toward A Metaphysics of Natural Coherence"; "Bipolar Co-Evolution: Outline of a Metaphysics of Universal Coherence"; and "The Next Creative Advance."

[23] Edwards, "How Process Philosophy Can Affirm Creation *Ex Nihilo*," 78–84.

[24] See Joseph A. Bracken's arguments in this regard in "Prehending God in and through the World," in ibid., 4–15.

[25] See Shoyo Taniguchi, "Modern Science and Early Buddhist Ethics: Methodology of Two Disciplines," 45–53.

[26] Paul Tillich, *Systematic Theology* (Chicago: University of Chicago Press, 1951) 1:235–92.

[27] For example, see John Cobb Jr., *God and the World* (Philadelphia: Westminster, 1969) chapter 2; and idem, *A Christian Natural Theology* (Philadelphia: Westminster, 1965) chapters 5–7.

[28] Barbour, *Religion and Science*, 77–105.

[29] See, for example, Mary Evelyn Tucker and Duncan Ryukan Williams, eds., *Buddhism and Ecology* (Cambridge: Harvard University Press, 1998); and three essays in J. Baird Callicott and Roger T. Ames, eds., *Nature in Asian Traditions of Thought* (Albany: SUNY Press, 1989) titled "The Jeweled Net of Indra" by Francis Cook (213–30), "Environmental Problems" by Kenneth K. Inada (231–46), and "Toward a Middle Path of Survival" by David J. Kaluphana (247–58).

[30] B. Alan Wallace, *Choosing Reality: A Buddhist View of Physics and the Mind*, chapter 11.

[31] Ibid., 14.

[32] Ibid., 9.

[33] Ibid.

[34] Ibid.

[35] Geoffrey Redmond, "Introduction," *The Pacific World* 11–12 (1995–96) 2–3. Also see "Comparing Science and Buddhism," ibid., 101–14.

[36] Victor Mansfield, "Time in Madhyamika Buddhism and Modern Physics," in ibid., 28–67.

[37] Shoyo Taniguchi, "Modern Science and Early Buddhist Ethics: Methodology of Two Disciplines," in ibid., 28–67.

[38] Denis Edwards, *The God of Evolution: A Trinitarian Theology* (New York: Paulist, 1999) chapter 1.

[39] Ibid., 13.

[40] Ibid., 15.

[41] Ibid., 41–42.

[42] See Ted Peter's review of Edwards book in *CTNS Bulletin* 19.3 (1999) 21.

[43] Denis Edwards, "A Brief Response to Peters," in ibid., 23.

[44] Frederick J. Streng, *Emptiness: A Study in Religious Meaning* (Nashville: Abingdon, 1967) chapters 2–3.

[45] Cf. Tucker and Williams, eds., *Buddhism and Ecology*; Christopher S. Queen and Sallie B. King, eds., *Engaged Buddhism: Buddhist Liberation Movements in Asia* (New York: SUNY Press, 1996); and Christopher S. Queen, ed., *Engaged Buddhism in the West* (Boston: Wisdom, 2000).

[46] See Kenneth R. Miller, *Finding Darwin's God: A Scientist's Search for Common Ground between God and Evolution* (New York: Cliff Street, 1999) 15.

[47] E. O. Wilson, *On Human Nature* (Cambridge: Harvard University Press, 1978) 1.

[48] Richard Dawkins, *River out of Eden* (New York: Harper Collins, 1995) 95–96.

[49] Steven Weinberg, *The First Three Minutes: A Modern View of the Origin of the Universe* (New York: Basic, 1988) 150–55.

[50] George C. Williams, *The Pony Fish's Glow* (New York: HarperCollins, 1997) 156–57, cited by Miller, *Finding Darwin's God*, 16.

Chapter 6

Is This All There Is?

Contemplating the past and thinking about the future is one of those "universals of human experience," as Joseph Campbell phrased it, that has defined what it means to be human since Cro-Magnons painted the shapes of animals on the walls of deep caves in France thousands of years ago. Knowing where we came from helps us understand where we are now, which in turn gives us hints about how we might anticipate the future. Mircea Eliade was right.[1] The construction of cosmologies—creation and origin myths that help us understand where we came from, where we are now, and where and how we might end up—are so pervasive across human history that one might be tempted to conclude that cosmological speculation is part of the human genetic code. In fact I do not know of a single religious tradition that does not structure its teachings, practices, and rituals according to some foundational cosmology. Cosmologies are one of the ways cultures and persons wrestle with God.

Traditional Buddhist cosmology is an origin story involving not only the life of the founder of Buddhism, Gautama, but also the origin of suffering and its resolution. As I noted in chapter five, the Buddhist worldview does not include a creation story about the beginning of the universe, which classical Buddhist cosmology assumes is eternal.

But Buddhist doctrines of karma and rebirth presuppose a cosmology according to which the universe is interpreted as a system of interdependent cycles whose spinning is directed by the Law of Karma. Thus while the interdependent events that constitute the universe are impermanent and interdependent, the universe that supports these events is eternal in the sense of always being in existence.

But the cosmological foundation of Judaism, Christianity, and Islam is a creation story. While this story has distinctive Jewish, Christian, and Islamic nuances, the Christian version of this story asserts that the universe originates in God's primal creative act, which God continues within the structures of natural processes until creation achieves God's intention, after which the universe as human beings know it will end and be replaced by a "new creation."

The origin of the universe according to contemporary scientific cosmology and evolutionary theory about the origin of life were the foci of chapter five, which considered the challenges posed by contemporary science to both Christian and Buddhist teachings and practices. Neither the Big Bang nor the Theory of Evolution are "fact" in any naive meaning of this word. But at this time they offer the most convincing theoretical explanations of the evolution of the universe and its life and are the best scientific approximations we currently have. Both theories may be proven wrong. More likely both will be unified and enfolded within a more comprehensive theory that will include a quantum theory of gravity.

However, my description of current scientific cosmology in chapter five was incomplete because it did not include speculation about the future of the universe that is now emerging in the natural sciences. Scientific speculation about the end of the universe in light of the Big Bang theory about its origins poses powerful challenges to all religious traditions and worldviews. Here's how.

In 1988 two groups of astrophysicists, one led by Brian Schmidt and the other by Saul Perlmutter, using similar techniques, were looking for a specific kind of explosion called a "Type 1a supernova," which occurs when an aging star destroys itself in a gigantic thermonuclear blast. Type 1a supernovas are so bright that their light can be seen all the way across the universe and is uniform enough to have its distance from Earth calculated with a great degree of accuracy. This is important because, as Edwin Hubbell discovered, the whole universe is expanding at a given rate at any time, which means that more distant galaxies are receding from Earth faster than nearby galaxies. So Schmidt's and Perlmutter's teams measured the distance to these supernovas (deduced from their brightness) and their speed of recession (deduced by the reddening of their light known as the Doppler shift).

When this information was finally gathered and analyzed, both teams knew something very quirky was going on. In the eighties, astrophysicists thought the universe's expansion would eventually slow down, either gradually or rapidly, depending on the amount of matter contained in the universe—an effect that was expected to show up as distant supernovas looking brighter than one would expect when compared to closer supernovas. But in fact these distant supernovas were dimmer, which meant that the universe's expansion was speeding up, which in turn suggested that some sort of powerful "dark energy" now called antigravity is forcing the galaxies to fly apart even as gravity draws them together. This means there is now more antigravity pushing the galaxies apart at an accelerating rate than there is gravity pulling the galaxies together. It follows that the universe will continue to expand forever unless forces now unknown to science are at work.

So given what cosmologists conclude about the universe's origins according to the Big Bang theory and the fact that the universe will most probably expand infinitely, a picture of the universe's final end seems to be emerging in the scientific community. The hundred billion or so galaxies that can now be observed through the Hubbell telescope and telescopes on Earth will zip out of range. Tens of billions of years from now, the Milky Way will be the only galaxy detectable from Earth, although it's unlikely anything will be alive on our planet by then. Other nearby galaxies, including the Large Magellanic Cloud and the Andromeda Galaxy, will have drifted into and merged with the Milky Way.

By this time, the sun will have shrunken to a white dwarf, giving little light and less heat to whatever is left on Earth, and will have entered into a long, lingering death that could last a hundred trillion years—or a thousand times longer than the universe has existed to this date. The same will happen to most other stars, although a few will end as blazing supernovas. Finally, all that will be left of the universe will be black holes, the burnt out residue of stars, and whatever remains of dead planets.

Even this is not the end, according to Fred Adams, a University of Michigan astrophysicist who has written much about the fate of the cosmos and is the co-author with Greg Laughlin of *The Five Ages of the Universe*.[2] Adams predicts that all the matter at this stage of the universe's evolution will collapse into black holes. By the time the universe is one trillion trillion trillion trillion trillion trillion years old, these black holes themselves will disintegrate into stray particles, which bind loosely enough to form individual "atoms" the size of today's universe. Eventually, even these will decay, leaving a featureless, infinitely large void. And that will be that—if this account of the universe's end is accurate or unless whatever inconceivable event that launched the original Big Bang should recur again.

Astronomers and physicists are members of a very cautious community, and they insist that the mind-bending discoveries about dark matter, dark energy, and the apparent flatness of space-time (which means the universe's shape is flat rather than curved) must be confirmed before they can be finally accepted. There could be more surprises to come: a cosmological constant—a notion Albert Einstein repudiated as his biggest mistake—is now the leading candidate for understanding dark energy. However, dark energy could be something altogether different, perhaps a force that could even reverse directions at some future point of space-time and reinforce rather than oppose gravity. If, however, these discoveries do hold up, some of the most important questions in cosmology—the universe's age, what it's made of, and how it will end—will be answered only seventy years after they were first posed. And well before the time cosmic history ends—further in the future than human minds can grasp—humanity, and perhaps even biology, will have vanished. Yet it is conceivable that consciousness of some sort may survive, perhaps in the form of a disembodied digital intelligence.[3] If so, this intelligence will notice that the universe, once ablaze with light from uncountable stars, has become a vast, cold, dark, and lonely void.

If this is really all there is, the universe indeed seems pointless and empty of value; and the metaphysical conclusions Steven Weinberg draws from Big Bang cosmology, Richard Dawkens' interpretation of evolutionary history, and E. O. Wilson's theories of social biology and genetic determinism appear as accurate descriptions of reality—the way things really are, as opposed to the way religious persons would like things to be. Christian, Jewish, and Islamic doctrines and practices—every one of them—are illusions having no basis in physical fact. So too Theravada and Mahayana Buddhist doctrines and practices, Hindu tradition, Confucian and Taoist traditions, as well as the primal traditions of Native Americans and other tribal cultures, are likewise illusory. None of humanity's religious ways can have any ontological correspondence to reality. This means that all theologies of religion—exclusivist, inclusivist, or pluralistic—are meaningless and the practice of interreligious dialogue as a form of theological reflection is reflection on ideas without ontological correspondence to anything that can actually exist. In short, wrestling with God is an illusion and a waste of energy.

Yet, as John Polkinghorne reminds us, scientific inquiry is very narrow and focused—it deals with bits and pieces of physical processes of nature that can be analyzed through repeatable experimental procedures described mathematically.[4] That is, the brilliant intellectual power and success of the natural sciences in revealing the physical processes of the universe, as well as the technological applications of scientific knowledge, come at the price of ignoring most of what human beings experience. For example, while the methodological reductionisms of physics can easily explain why we hear sounds as the vibration of our ear drums at the impact of air molecules, physics cannot explain my or anyone else's love of jazz or classical music or the poetry of William Butler Yeats or T. S. Eliot, or why people prefer other styles of music or other poets. While biology can accurately explain the evolutionary history of the human eye, it cannot explain why the alternating light show of the Pacific Northwest on an autumn day, when the sun breaks through slate gray rain clouds and paints the trees in acrylic fall colors, always stuns me to silence. From the wider parameters of human experience, the reductionisms of scientists like Steven Weinberg, E. O. Wilson, and Richard Dawkins seem like incoherent metaphysics rather than scientific description.

It is also a fact that none of the religious traditions of humanity assume that scientific theoretical constructions and descriptions of physical reality describe "all there is." As John Hick never tires of pointing out, all religious human beings share a common "religious intention" not to delude themselves about the way things really are in this universe,[5] which is not to say that religious persons do not often delude themselves. Karl Marx was partly right. Religious faith and practice can be and often is an opiate, an anesthesia that deadens one's intellect and emotions, a prophylactic to shield oneself from contamination from the disagreeable realities of existence or from religious traditions, cultures, and people one regards as "other."

But Marx was also partly wrong. Historically, the most creative human advances are in what the Chinese called *wen* or the "arts" that civilize human beings. It is the arts, culture in its widest meanings, that place persons in contact with reality and with what is distinctive about being human. The arts of all cultures evolved from and are grounded in the religious traditions of those cultures. For example, the brilliance of Chinese culture during the T'ang and Sung dynasties was rooted in Confucian and Buddhist sources; the European Renaissance owes its beginnings to the Islamic culture of the House of Wisdom in twelfth-century Damascus and Andalusian Spain; and the art, music, and political and economic philosophy of Europe, as well as the natural sciences, have their theological and philosophical foundations in Jewish, Christian, and Islamic thought.

Surely, the experiences and teachings of the Buddha, Mohammed's experience as a messenger called to recite God's words to his people, the historical Jesus' experience of the Kingdom of God and God's call to enter this kingdom in obedience to the demands of radical love, Hindu experience of Brahman as one's deepest Self, Confucius' sensitivity to the moral foundations of the natural order, or the experiences of sacred power in the forces of nature in native American experience are not collective illusions. I cannot prove it, but I find it difficult to believe that collective illusions can hang around in human history for as long as Buddhism, Christianity, Islam, Hinduism, Confucianism, and Native American cultures have endured. Human beings are often collectively and individually stupid, but probably not for as long as the world's religious traditions have existed.

Nevertheless, if it is confirmed that the universe's expansion continues forever, the universe, in fact, seems condemned to futility, and human existence is a transient episode in its history. Such a bleak prognosis of the universe's destiny certainly puts in question the evolutionary optimism of such writers as Teilhard de Chardin, who posits a final fulfillment of existence solely within the confines of the unfolding of physical processes into a final "Omega point."[6] Such notions seem particularly irrelevant given what physicists are now understanding about the universe's origins and destiny.

Still, neither the Bible nor mainline Christian theological reflection and practice stakes its claims on the foundations of evolutionary optimism or scientific description of physical fact. The issue is a metaphysical one. Hope that "this isn't all there is" will have to be grounded in an ultimate reality, not on scientific description of physical processes, even though theological reflection must be contextualized by what the sciences tell us about these processes. In Christian language, this ultimate reality is named God. Hope that the universe is not pointless will have to rest on God, not in the universe God creates and sustains, but apparently not forever.

Since Buddhist non-theism has not as yet entered conceptual dialogue with the natural sciences on the final destiny of the universe, dialogue with Buddhism cannot aid Christian theological reflection on the possibility of universe's final fulfillment. In Christian tradition, this form of theological reflection is called "eschatology," meaning "reflection on the final destiny of the cosmos." Accordingly, the remainder of this chapter steps out of dialogical encounter with Buddhist tradition by asking the following eschatological question: what are the grounds for hope that "this isn't all there is"?

What follows is based on three assumptions. First, the eventual futility of the universe over a time scale of many trillions of years is not, it seems to me, different from the theological problem this fact poses for the eventual futility of ourselves over a time scale of tens of years. Human death, indeed the death of all living things, is a mirror of the cosmic death the universe itself will undergo in the distant future. Death is built into the structure of existence because of the Second Law of Thermodynamics, which asserts that in an isolated system (galaxies, stars, planets, animals, plants, us) insulated from external influence things tend to become more disorderly. In other words, existence is terminal. Both cosmic death and human death, as well as the death of all non-human life forms, pose equivalent questions about the nature of God's intention for the universe. Since, according to Jewish, Christian, and Islamic teaching, God is the creator of the universe and its laws, including the Second Law of Thermodynamics, the theological issue is the faithfulness of God, the constant and everlasting seriousness with which God regards all creatures that have lived, now live, or will ever live.

Second, evidence that God is faithful will not be found through scientific inquiry because of the narrowness of both the object of scientific investigation and the practice of scientific method. As God cannot rightly be brought into scientific investigation as a "God of the gaps" to plug up holes in scientific theory, the conclusions of science cannot rightly be employed to plug up the "gaps" of theological theory.

So is there a purpose at the bottom of existence? Is the universe against us, indifferent to us, or perhaps for us? When such questions are put to nature, the answer is usually silence. Yet every once in a while, science stumbles on a clue, like the anthropic principle, that suggests that maybe the universe had observers like us in mind from the first moment of the Big Bang.

Perhaps. But it would be foolish to take the anthropic principle as proof for the existence of God, even if it might make belief in God reasonable.[7] Besides, scientific method cancels out speculation about God from its conclusions. When all is said and done, in response to questions like "is this all there is?" science must remain mute. Stated bluntly, the reasonableness of the hope that God is faithful and that this isn't all there is must rest on wider forms of experience that are not accessible to scientific inquiry, but which are, nevertheless, as real as the physical processes the natural sciences seek to understand. Consequently, while I shall be reflecting from the context of Christian experience, this should not be interpreted to mean that I think Christian faith and practice provide the only valid clues to what is theologically going on in human experience or in the universe.

Third, I do not know how the universe began and neither do contemporary cosmologists. Any scientific cosmological theory—the current one being the Big Bang—that tries to tell us about what happened near the origin of the universe is going to assume that the laws of nature already existed. But at the instant of the Big Bang singularity, no laws of nature existed that physicists can identify, which does not mean that physicists might not be able to do so in the future. So my question is, where do the laws of nature that physics assert break down at the singularity of the Big Bang come from? My answer—a theological answer, not a scientific one—is God. I think the Creator allows the history of the universe to unfold from the singularity of the Big Bang, which means the universe doesn't come from nothing. It comes out of the laws of nature created by God.

For me, the question of the beginning and ending of existence for all things and events caught in the field of space-time is most meaningfully portrayed in the Gospel of Mark's account of Jesus' argument with the Sadducees about the resurrection of the dead: "As for the dead being raised, have you not read in the book of Moses, in the passage about the bush, how God said to him, 'I am the God of Abraham, and the God of Isaac, and the God of Jacob?' He is not God of the dead, but of the living." (Mark 12:26-27) In other words, God did not abandon the Hebrew patriarchs once they served their purpose, but had an eternal destiny for them. Likewise, God does not abandon the universe and its life forms once the universe and its life forms have served their purpose.

But how credible is such hope given what physics and biology tell us about the physical processes of the universe? Although there are strands of Christian tradition that affirm the survival of an immortal soul entity after death, I think the tradition that comes closest to what the sciences reveal about the natural order is the New Testament's vision of the hope of resurrection beyond death. In this context, the issue in not one of surviving death because of the existence of an intrinsically immortal soul or self-entity that remains self-identical through time. My understanding of selfhood is very much influenced by Buddhist notions of non-self, which has also opened up my understanding of Biblical notions of selfhood, as well as of Whiteheadian process theology's account of selfhood.[8] Neither the human self, nor any other form of selfhood, is permanent. Existence is characterized by impermanence because of the Second Law of Thermodynamics. In this, Buddhist teaching, Biblical tradition, and process theology are in agreement.

According to the categories of Whiteheadian process thought, the human self, and the selves of whatever other life forms experience degrees of conscious self-awareness, is a complex, dynamic, information bearing-pattern that is physically embodied at any instant in the complex societies of actual occasions that constitute the physical body. The self exhibits its own "subjective aim" to achieve the maximum fulfillment or "satisfaction" it can, given the physical and historical contexts in which it finds itself and which it must take into account. But the self is also "lured" by God's "initial aim" that its subjective aim be in harmony with God's aim that all entities achieve their own final fulfillment in interdependence with each other. In the complex life form that is a human being, the self's subjective aim and God's initial aim for the self are usually in conflict, but both operate in the self's becoming. According to John Cobb, what made the historical Jesus so extraordinary was that Jesus' subjective aim and God's initial aim for Jesus were non-dual.[9] Or in more traditional Christian language, Jesus subordinated his will to the will of God.

The psychosomatic unity of the self and its physical embodiment is dissolved at death, but I think it is coherent to hope that the pattern that is me, as well as the pattern of all living things, from the moment of conception to the moment of death, is remembered (in Whitehead's word, "prehended") and reconstituted by God in a new environment of God's choosing, which is what I understand to be the meaning of St. Paul's teaching about the resurrection:

> What I am saying, brothers and sisters, is this: flesh and blood cannot inherit the Kingdom of God, nor does the perishable inherit the imperishable. Listen, I will tell you a mystery. We will not all die, but we will all be changed, in a moment, in the twinkling of an eye, at the last trumpet. For the trumpet will sound, and the dead will be raised imperishable, and we will be changed. (1 Cor 15:50-52)

In other words, life is embodied in physical processes; all life is embodied life. Whatever hope can reasonably exist that death is not all there is lies in the resurrection of the body. By this I do not mean the resuscitation of our present physical structure. In physicist-theologian John Polkinghorne's "crude analogy":

> The software running on our present hardware will be transferred to the hardware of the world to come. And where will that eschatological hardware come from? Surely the "matter" of the world to come must be transformed matter of this world. God will no more abandon the universe than he will abandon us. Hence the importance to theology of the empty tomb, with its message that the Lord's risen and glorified body is the transmutation of his dead body.[10]

"It is in the resurrection of Jesus," Polkinghorne continues in his interpretation of Romans 8:18-25, that "the destiny of humanity and the destiny of the universe together find their mutual fulfillment in a liberation from decay and futility."[11]

This picture of a cosmic redemption in which a resurrected humanity will participate is "as immensely thrilling as it is immensely mysterious."[12] Still, such an unimaginable future reflects an almost universal hope that, all the ambiguities and suffering of history notwithstanding, in the end all will be well. Historically, such hope is so widely prevalent as to constitute what Peter Berger calls a "signal of transcendence."[13] It is important that Christians not lose their nerve in witnessing to this "signal."

Consequently, in the community of faith called the Church, Christians know the present for what it is—a point of time too charged with eternity to be understood except through mythic and poetic language. By this I mean language drawn from biblical imagery, two thousand years of Christian theological reflection, the experience of worship, art, music, social engagement, and the practice of interreligious dialogue. It is the only way we can reflect on that which we have not experienced while we are alive. For the problem is that no one alive knows *what* death is, only *that* death is, because we can only know by means of rational reflection on what we experience. But by the time we experience death, it may be too late to reflect rationally on the experience.

The need to use mythic and poetic language in order to speak of what we have not yet experienced must not engender the illusory comfort of fables. For Christians, this means betting one's life on, that is, trusting, being faithful to, the historical Jesus as the Christ. Such faith need not imply that only Christians experience resurrection or that, whatever resurrection is, it occurred in history for the first time at the resurrection of the historical Jesus. Here is how David Toolan expresses it:

In hindsight, the church has understood Jesus in cosmic terms. As the New Testament testifies, Jesus has to be taken as a prototype of our species and, better yet, in cosmic-ecological terms, as the archetype of what the quarks and the molecules, from the beginning, were predestined to become—one resurrected body. Jesus is not simply a moral example. He is, as St. Paul would have it, the axis of cosmic time and the prototype of the fullest embodiment of our species' role: the carrier and vessel, the fleshing out of the Creator's great dream for the universe.[14]

The two primary sources for this understanding are St. Paul and the writer of the Gospel of John. For them, the doctrine of creation had a central importance: As the Gospel of John has it, "In the beginning was the Word, and the Word was with God and the Word was God. . . . and without him was not anything made that was made" (John 1:1-3). In this sense, the creation of the universe entails the doctrine of redemption. Or, to put it another way, creation and salvation are interdependent. To the original Jewish followers of Jesus, this must have sounded as if God's Torah or "instructions" had surfaced in the words of a man, because in hearing Jesus they apprehended the voice of the Creator. The primordial Word was "made flesh, he lived among us, and we saw his glory. . . . full of grace and truth" (John 1:14). So the Christian claim is that a minority of one in a backwater region of the Roman Empire altered the course of the universe's history.

However, if God is ultimately the source of all that is because the laws of nature originated with God, we need to ask about the reality of evil and suffering. If God *is* love, as 1 John 4:16 notes, and God's love is the power that energizes the whole universe, the problem of evil is the most difficult of theological questions for Christians, Jews, and Muslims. And while non-theistic religious traditions do not encounter the problem of evil in the form of "theodocy" or the "justification of God," the fact of universal suffering raises important issues for all religious traditions. Suffering is real—for all sentient beings—and those in pain know it.

The form of the question for Christians is why does God's power that is love allow evil and suffering? It's rough out there in the universe, where the survival of any species of life entails the suffering and death of countless species of life. In our universe, life *must* eat life to survive. Furthermore, human beings have brought suffering not only to other human beings but to nature itself.

If God's power is best understood as love—Whitehead would say that God's power as love works as a divine "lure" that "persuades" all things and events to achieve their fullest "satisfaction" as all things and events contribute to the ongoing creative process and to God's own experience—then God is not a cosmic tyrant who predestines events before they happen. Love for God and for us happens in relationships, none of which we experience as permanent, that recognize the independence and interdependence of that which is loved.

In other words, from electrons to human beings, God structures freedom into the universe itself. Freedom may be trivial at the sub-atomic level, but for human beings it is not. Human beings are free to reject God's lure to live in mutually interdependent fulfillment with each other and with nature, which means God will not stop a murderer from shooting his weapon or prevent the Holocaust or genocide in Rwanda. Here, Luther's "theology of the cross" provides an instructive approach: God interacts with the world, shares the world's suffering with us, and redeems what can be redeemed from the mess we make as well as from the suffering that the processes of evolution naturally entail. But God does not control everything, because love means allowing the beloved freedom to not respond to love that is offered.

At this point, the natural sciences can again inform theological reflection. The more physics and biology reveal about the universe, the more it looks like a package deal. While human beings make contributions to the creative process even as we add to the natural suffering already ingredient in existence, we also tend to think that if we were in charge of the universe, we would keep all the good and throw away the bad. But neither the universe, nor anything else, can be divided so dualistically. For example, contemporary evolutionary theory shows how genetic mutation has driven the evolutionary history of life on Earth, eventually transforming bacteria into human beings. Genetic mutation is a great good, but this same process allows some cells to become malignant. So the evolution of life cannot happen without cancer, which causes terrible suffering.

Freeman Dyson notes something very similar in the concluding paragraphs of his *Origins of Life*.[15] There is a "sloppiness" to life, he notes, in which life must be able to tolerate error in order to be robust. Novelty happens at the edge of chaos, so that if something is too stable, too robust, it's just rigid and nothing new happens. If something is too chaotic, it falls apart. It's in that edge, that sloppy region where openness is joined to preservation, that life really happens. This region is a necessarily dangerous place, but not because God is careless or incompetent. It's just the cost of the great fruitfulness we call "life."

I think something like this idea lies behind St. Paul's portrayal of Jesus as the Christ:

> He is the image of the invisible God, the first born of all creation; for in him all things were created, in heaven and on earth, visible and invisible. . . . he is the beginning, the first born from the dead, that in everything he might be permanent. For in him all the fullness of God was pleased to dwell, and through him to reconcile to himself all things, whether in earth or in heaven. (Col 1:15-20)

Or as Cobb interprets the structure of experience that defines Christian experience and faith:

> The structure of experience with Christ which is bound up with hope in history is that of dying and rising. Each moment, as soon as it is realized, itself perishes or dies. The new moment truly lives only as it finds some novel possibility that is its own, appropriate to its unique situation, and worthy of realization in its own right. Living from our past instead is not a real option. If we seek life by clinging to past realizations, we do not live at all. It is only a question of the pace of death. The one who holds to the past and repeats it does not enliven the past but only joins it in death. However, the one who turns from the past in openness to the new finds the past restored and revitalized. . . . It is when we think new thoughts that our past thinking remains a vital contributing element, not when we endlessly repeat ourselves or try to defend what we thought in the past.[16]

In other words, it is by dying that we live. Whatever redemption is, it encompasses more than humanity, past, present, or future; redemption encompasses the whole natural order, every thing and event in the universe since the first instant of the Big Bang until the physical processes of this universe finally play out trillions of years into the future. For, as St. Paul put it, "God was in Christ reconciling the world to himself." (2 Cor 5:19) The deepest meaning of the universe, the meaning of fourteen billion years of evolution and beyond, is that all of nature every thing and event caught in the field of space-time—past, present, and future—is always united to God. Nothing is left out that can be included. Absolutely nothing.

ENDNOTES

[1] See Mircea Eliade, *The Sacred and the Profane: The Nature of Religion*, trans. Williard R. Trask (New York: Harcourt Brace, 1957) chapters 1 and 2.

[2] Fred Adams and Greg Laughlin, *The Five Ages of the Universe* (New York: Touchstone, 2000).

[3] See Frank J. Tipler, "The Omega Point as *Eschaton*: Answers to Pannenberg's Questions for Scientists," *Zygon* 24 (1989) 217–53; idem, "The Omega Point Theory: A Model for an Evolving God," in *Physics, Philosophy, and Theology*, ed. Robert J. Russell et al. (Vatican City: Vatican Observatory, 1988) and *Physics of Immortality* (New York: Doubleday, 1994).

[4] John Polkinghorne, *Belief in God in an Age of Science* (New Haven: Yale University Press, 1998) chapter 2.

[5] John Hick, *An Interpretation of Religion: Human Responses to the Transcendent* (New Haven: Yale University Press, 1989) chapter 11.

[6] Teilhard de Chardin, *The Phenomenon of Man*, trans. Bernard Wall (New York: Collins, 1959).

[7] James Kraft, "The Anthropic as a Source of Interreligious Dialogue," *CTNS Bulletin* 20 (Winter 2000) 14–18.

[8] Paul O. Ingram, *The Modern Buddhist-Christian Dialogue* (New York: Mellen, 1988) chapter 7.

[9] John B. Cobb Jr., *Christ in a Pluralistic Age* (Philadelphia: Westminster, 1975) 97–110.

[10] John Polkinghorne, *The Faith of a Physicist* (Minneapolis: Fortress, 1996) 164.

[11] Ibid.

[12] Ibid.

[13] Peter L. Berger, *A Rumor of Angels: Modern Society and the Rediscovery of the Supernatural* (Garden City, N.Y.: Doubleday, 1969) 72–76.

[14] David Toolan, *At Home in the Cosmos* (Maryknoll, N.Y.: Orbis, 2001) 208.

[15] Freeman Dyson, *Origins of Life*, rev. ed. (Cambridge: Cambridge University Press, 1999).

[16] Cobb, *Christ in a Pluralistic Age*, 243.

Selected Bibliography

Abe, Masao, and John B. Cobb Jr. "Buddhist-Christian Dialogue: Past, Present, Future." *Buddhist-Christian Studies* 1 (1981) 13–30.

Adams, Fred, and Greg Laughlin. *The Five Ages of the Universe: Inside the Physics of Eternity*. New York: Free Press, 1999.

Barbour, Ian. *Religion and Science: Historical and Contemporary Issues*. Rev. ed. San Francisco: HarperCollins, 1997.

Berger, Peter L. *A Rumor of Angels: Modern Society and the Rediscovery of the Supernatural*. Garden City, N.Y.: Doubleday, 1969.

Callicott, J. Baird, and Roger T. Ames, editors. *Nature in Asian Traditions of Thought: Essays in Environmental Philosophy*. SUNY Series in Philosophy and Biology. Albany, N.Y.: SUNY Press, 1989.

Ch'en, Kenneth K. S. *Buddhism in China: A Historical Survey*. Princeton, N.J.: Princeton University Press, 1979.

Cobb, John B., Jr. "Can a Christian Be a Buddhist, Too?" *Japanese Religions* 10 (1979) 1–20.

———. *Christ in a Pluralistic Age*. 1979. Reprinted, Eugene, Ore.: Wipf & Stock, 1998.

———. *The Structure of Christian Existence*. Philadelphia: Westminster, 1972.

———. "Global Theology in a Pluralistic Age." In *Transforming Christianity and the World*, edited by Paul F. Knitter. Maryknoll, N.Y.: Orbis, 1999.

Cross, John Dominic. *The Dark Interval: Toward a Theology of Story*. Sonoma, Calif.: Polebridge, 1988.

Daly, Herman E., and John B.Cobb Jr., with Clifford W. Cobb. *For the Common Good: Redirecting the Economy toward Community, the Environment, and a Sustainable Future*. 2d ed. Boston: Beacon, 1994.

Dawkins, Richard. *River Out of Eden: A Darwinian View of Life*. New York: Basic Books, 1995.

D'Costa, Gavin, ed. *Christian Uniqueness Reconsidered: The Myth of a Pluralistic Theology of Religions*. Faith Meets Faith. Maryknoll, N.Y.: Orbis, 1990.

Dillard, Anne. *Pilgrim at Tinker Creek*. New York: Harper and Row, 1974.

Dreyfus, George. "Meditation as Ethical Activity." *Journal of Buddhist Ethics* 2 (1995) 31–44. [Online]. Available FTP: ftp.cac.psu.edu Directory: JBE2/1995 File: dreyfus.txt.

Dumoulin, Henrich, and John C. Naraldo, editors. *Buddhism in the Modern World*. New York: Macmillan, 1978.

Dunne, John S. *The Way of All the Earth: Experiments in Truth and Religion*. Notre Dame: University of Notre Dame Press, 1978.

Dyson, Freeman. *Origins of Life*. Rev. ed. Cambridge: Cambridge University Press, 1999.

Edwards, Denis. *The God of Evolution: A Trinitarian Theology*. New York: Paulist, 1999.

Edwards, Rem B. "How Process Philosophy Can Affirm Creation *Ex Nihilo*." *Process Studies* 29 (Spring-Summer 2000) 77–98.

Eisley, Loren. *The Unexpected Universe*. New York: Harcourt, 1969.

Eliade, Mircea. *The Sacred and the Profane: The Nature of Religion*. Translated by Willard R. Trask. New York: Harcourt, Brace, 1959.

Gilkey, Langdon. *Nature, Reality, and the Sacred: The Nexus of Science and Religion*. Theology and the Sciences. Minneapolis: Fortress, 1993.

Harvey, Van A. *The Historian and the Believer: The Morality of Historical Knowledge and Christian Belief*. New York: Macmillan, 1966.

Hawking, Stephen W. *A Brief History of Time: From the Big Bang to Black Holes*. New York: Bantam, 1988.

Hetherington, Norriss S. *Cosmology: Historical, Literary, Philosophical, Religious, and Scientific Perspectives*. New York: Garland, 1993.

Hick, John. *A Christian Theology of Religions*. Louisville: Westminster John Knox, 1995.

———. *An Interpretation of Religion: Human Responses to the Transcendent*. New Haven: Yale University Press, 1989.

Ingram, Paul O. *The Dharma of Faith*. Washington, D.C.: University Press of America, 1977.

———. *The Modern Buddhist-Christian Dialogue: Two Universalistic Religions in Transformation*. Studies in Comparative Religion 2. Lewiston, N.Y.: Mellen, 1988.

———. "Buddhism and Christian Theology." In *The Modern Theologians*, edited by David F. Ford, 682–702. Oxford: Blackwell, 2005.

———. "Shinran Shonin and Martin Luther: A Soteriological Comparison." *Journal of the American Academy of Religion* 39 (1971) 447–80.

———. "'That We May Know Each Other': The Pluralist Hypothesis as a Research Program." *Buddhist-Christian Studies* 24 (2004) 138–57.

———. *Wrestling With the Ox: A Theology of Religious Experience*. New York: Continuum, 1997.

Bibliography

Ingram, Paul O., and Frederick J. Streng, editors. *Buddhist-Christian Dialogue: Mutual Renewal and Transformation*. Honolulu: University of Hawaii Press, 1986.

Keating, Thomas. *Open Mind, Open Heart: The Contemplative Dimension of the Gospel*. New York: Continuum, 1995.

Keenan, John P. *The Gospel of Mark: A Mahayana Interpretation*. Faith Meets Faith. Maryknoll, N.Y.: Orbis, 1995.

Killen, Patricia O'Connell, and John de Beer. *The Art of Theological Reflection*. New York: Crossroad, 1994.

King, Sallie B., and Paul O. Ingram, editors. *The Sound of Liberating Truth: Buddhist-Christian Dialogues in Honor of Frederick J. Streng*. Curzon Critical Studies in Religion. Richmond, Surrey: Curzon, 1999.

King, Sallie B., and Christopher Queen, editors. *Engaged Buddhism: Buddhist Liberation Movements in Asia*. Albany, N.Y.: SUNY Press, 1996.

King, Winston L. *In the Hope of Nibbana: An Essay on Theravada Buddhist Ethics*. La Salle, Ill.: Open Court, 1964.

Knitter, Paul F. *Jesus and the Other Names: Christian Mission and Global Responsibility*. Maryknoll, N.Y.: Orbis, 1996.

Kraft, James. "The Anthropic Principle as a Source of Interreligious Dialogue." *CTNS Bulletin* 20 (Winter 2000) 14–18.

Kraft, Kenneth, editor. *Inner Peace, World Peace: Essays on Buddhism and Nonviolence*. SUNY Series in Buddhist Studies. Albany, N.Y.: SUNY Press, 1992.

Lasswell, Harold D., and Harlan Cleveland, editors. *The Ethic of Power: The Interplay of Religion, Philosophy, and Politics*. New York: Harper, 1962.

Merton, Thomas. *Entering the Silence: Becoming a Monk & Writer*. The Journals of Thomas Merton. Edited by Jonathan Montaldo. San Francisco: Harper, 1996.

Miller, Kenneth R. *Finding Darwin's God: A Scientist's Search for Common Ground between God and Evolution*. New York: Cliff Street, 1999.

Moltmann, Jürgen. *The Source of Life: The Holy Spirit and the Theology of Life*. Translated by Margaret Kohl. Minneapolis: Fortress, 1997.

Newbigin, Lesslie. *The Gospel in a Pluralistic Society*. Grand Rapids: Eerdmans, 1989.

Nhat Hanh, Thich. *Being Peace*. Edited by Arnold Kotler. Berkeley: Parallax, 1989.

———. *Living Buddha, Living Christ*. Berkeley: Riverhead, 1995.

———. *Lotus in a Sea of Fire*. London: SCM, 1961.

Peacocke, Arthur. *Theology for a Scientific Age: Being and Becoming—Natural, Divine and Human*. Minneapolis: Fortress, 1993.

Polkinghorne, John. *Belief in God in an Age of Science*. The Terry Lectures. New Haven: Yale University Press, 1998.

———. *The Faith of a Physicist*. Minneapolis: Fortress, 1993.

Porete, Marguerite. *The Mirror of Simple Souls*. Translated and introduced by Ellen L. Babinsky. New York: Paulist, 1993.

Prebish, Charles S. "Test and Tradition in the Study of Buddhist Ethics." *Pacific World* 9 (1993) 49–68.

Prebish, Charles S., and Kenneth K. Tanaka, editors. *The Faces of Buddhism in America*. Berkeley: University of California Press, 1998.

Queen, Christopher S., editor. *Engaged Buddhism in the West*. Boston: Wisdom, 2000.

Ruether, Rosemary Radford. *Faith and Fratricide: The Theological Roots of Anti-Semiticism*. 1979. Reprinted, Eugene, Ore.: Wipf & Stock, 1996.

Schillebeeckx, Edward. *The Church: The Human Story of God*. Translated by John Bowden. New York: Crossroad, 1990.

Sizemore, Russell F., and Donald Swearer, editors. *Ethics, Wealth, and Salvation: A Study in Buddhist Social Ethics*. Studies in Comparative Religion. Columbia: University of South Carolina Press, 1992.

Smith, Wilfred Cantwell. *Faith and Belief*. Princeton: Princeton University Press, 1979.

Streng, Frederick J. *Emptiness: A Study in Religious Meaning*. Nashville: Abingdon, 1967.

Taniguchi, Shoyo. "Modern Science and Early Buddhist Ethics: Methodology of Two Disciplines." *Pacific World* 11–12 (1995–96) 28–67.

Thurman, Robert A. F., translator. *The Holy Teaching of Vimalakīrti*. University Park: Pennsylvania State University Press, 1976.

Tipler, Frank J. *The Physics of Immortality: Modern Cosmology, God, and the Resurrection of the Dead*. New York: Doubleday, 1994.

———. "The Omega Point as Eschaton: Answers to Pannenberg's Questions for Scientists." *Zygon* 24 (1989) 217–53.

———. "The Omega Point Theory: A Model for an Evolving God." In *Physics, Philosophy, and Theology: A Common Quest for Understanding*, edited by Robert J. Russell et al., 313–31. Vatican City: Vatican Observatory, 1988.

Toolan, David. *At Home in the Cosmos*. Maryknoll, N.Y.: Orbis, 2001.

Traer, Robert. "Faith in the Buddhist Tradition." *Buddhist-Christian Studies* 11 (1991) 85–120.

Tucker, Mary Evelyn, and Duncan Ryukan Williams, editors. *Buddhism and Ecology: The Interconnection of Dharma and Deeds*. Religions of the World and Ecology. Cambridge: Harvard University Press, 1997.

Wallace, B. Allan. *Choosing Reality: A Buddhist View of Physics and the Mind*. Ithaca, N.Y.: Snow Lion, 1996.

Weinberg, Steven. *The First Three Minutes: A Modern View of the Origin of the Universe*. New York: Basic, 1977.

Whitehead, Alfred North. *Process and Reality: An Essay in Cosmology*. New York: Macmillan, 1957.

Williams, George C. *The Pony Fish's Glow: And Other Clues to Plan and Purpose in Nature*. Science Masters. New York: Basic, 1997.

Wilson, E. O. *On Human Nature*. Cambridge: Harvard University Press, 1978.